Testimonials

I first bought *How to Become a Professional Con Artist* hoping to discover why a cop would tell people how to commit fraud. Having read the book, I must now ask why he didn't write it sooner.

—Bonnie Hillmar, Bessemer, Michigan

Curiosity first prompted me to read *How to Become a Professional Con Artist*. Once read, utter disbelief kept me reading it over and over again.

—Edward Reid, Tulsa, Oklahoma

Although I have been a police fraud investigator for 20 years, *How to Become a Professional Con Artist* was a real eye-opener and an adventure I won't soon forget.

—Captain R.T. Walstad, Prairie Hills, Wisconsin

After reading *How to Become a Professional Con Artist*, I now realize that there is a world of difference between working hard and working intelligently.

—Reginald Hollister, London, England

How to Become a Professional Con Artist is an instant classic!

—Hannah Marie Masters, Rockport, Maine

As a law professor, I have read countless books, articles, and dissertations on fraud and deception. This, however, is the first time I have elected to endorse any author's work. *How to Become a Professional Con Artist* is indeed an academic gem worthy of inclusion in university curriculums throughout the nation.

—Henry Riordan, Ph.D., Seattle, Washington

This book is dedicated to those who have fallen prey to the deceivers of our world, and to the law enforcement officers, private citizens, and others who have dedicated themselves to beating the cons at their own game.

ACKNOWLEDGMENTS

Many names of people, places, and business firms have been changed to protect the author. If during this endeavor I have accidentally inserted your name, please forgive me.

A special thanks to John Dowling for his guidance throughout the writing of this book, and to Kathy Wirtes, who edited this work. My sincere gratitude.

TABLE OF CONTENTS

PREFACE

Confident in the knowledge I have obtained about your personal habits from our nation's con artists, I will forgo the hooks and gimmicks normally used to con you into a book purchase. Such influential trickery is unnecessary because, whether you realize it or not, your decision has already been made. In other words, you now possess a book titled *How to Become a Professional Con Artist.*

You could immediately prove me wrong by placing this book back onto the shelf, but for reasons you don't yet understand, this is no longer an option. Attempt to resist and you shall only cause yourself to suffer undue aggravation and a return trip to obtain this book. For now, please accept your inability to exercise free will on a bewitchment of your intelligence through the most powerful weapon on this planet, our language.

To illustrate the importance of the information contained within these pages and to offer proof of my deceptive honesty, here's something to consider. The easiest people to deceive are those who think themselves immune to all but the greatest of deceptions. Should this include you, here's a promise: To enhance your learning experience, I will deceive you whenever the opportunity arises. In fact, I already have. And I am confident that you don't know how or when this occurred.

Perhaps you believe the deception involves my promise to reveal the secrets of professional con artists. After all, a cop who for more than three decades has made life miserable for con artists wouldn't dare commit such a foolhardy act. Therefore, the title must be a lie. If you share in this belief, then Chapter One will displace any such notion. It's where you will learn how to help unsuspecting cashiers hand over much more change than you are due by using a technique called change raising.

My real act of deception involves those wonderful testimonials at the beginning of the book. I wholeheartedly agree with each of them for many reasons, but mostly because I wrote them.

There was, of course, no easy way for you to verify the accuracy of such material. But that's the point. Because we live in an information-laden, decision-overloaded environment, we are forever searching for shortcuts to help us avoid the time and trouble involved with research and thinking. The customized shortcut I provided simply took advantage of our tendency to make decisions based on what we believe others like us are doing. Having benefited from these thought-saving tactics in the past, seldom do we consciously realize how easy we have made it for those who wish to deceive us. The secrets behind these psychological ploys are revealed elsewhere in this book.

That I would dare tell you the secrets that go into the making of every successful confidence crime ever committed is no real mystery. Having written numerous fraud-prevention articles and two books, and having given countless crime prevention presentations to citizen and law enforcement groups, I fully expected to see a measurable drop in the incidence of fraud. After obtaining the long-awaited results I realized my time would have been better spent seeking a cure for hiccups. To demonstrate the extent of my ineffectiveness, here's a brief quote from a *Reader's Digest* article:

> "Every day thousands of Americans are tricked out of money they can't afford to lose. There are hundreds of schemes and rackets and any one of them may find its way to your door."

Within the past year, you have no doubt heard about or read hundreds of similar reports. What sets the *Digest* article apart is that it was published in July 1955. Other than the date, the only significant changes involve an increase in both the frequency of fraudulent activity and of our peculiar tolerance of those who openly deceive us.

I was reminded of such foolishness when actor Bill Paxton, promoting his appearance in the film *Traveller*, thought it appropriate to publicly applaud the activities of a group of organized con artists known as the Travellers; thieves who specialize in home-improvement, roofing, and driveway-repair scams. In a 1997 article written by Allan Johnson, a reporter for *The Chicago Tribune*, Paxton was quoted as saying, "Con artists are basically part of the American experience." He continued, "I think that this country was basically built by salesmen and confidence men." Such nonsense is what made this book possible.

If we insist on allowing the con artists of our world easy access to our families, our friends, and us, then we should at least get to know them. Not the watered-down Hollywood versions, but the real personalities that make it possible for them to work their scams. Only after such an examination can we intelligently decide whether joining their ranks is in our best interest.

Carefully dissect what the con artists have to offer, take part in the exercises, resist the urge to hurry your education by skipping chapters, and by journey's end you will know how to think, act, and rationalize like a true professional. Never again will you ask how any particular scam could possibly work, or why we have come to admire and trust people who view and treat us like idiots.

If you experience anger or disgust during your excursion, it's because you have resorted to viewing life through your own experiences rather than the con artist's. Allow this to cloud your thinking and you shall forever occupy the status of a doormat for use by those who know you better than you know yourself.

That you should want to become a professional swindler after reading this book is unlikely, yet possible. If you decide to test your newfound skills, please spare yourself the embarrassment of using *How to Become a Professional Con Artist* as a justification for your actions until you have read all that has been written. Choose to ignore this warning and you shall indeed become the world's dumbest criminal. And that's the truth.

CHAPTER ONE

CHANGE RAISING

*"Half the world is composed of idiots, the other half of
people clever enough to take indecent advantage of them."*
—Walter Kerr

Still not convinced of my promise to transform you into
a professional con artist? Then here are the details you'll
need to turn a quick profit. Wrongfully labeled as a shortchange, this particular money-making gimmick involves
an art form called change raising. The game works like this:

Buy a low-priced item, usually something for
under $1. Give the cashier a $10 bill.

When the cashier hands back your change, say
something like, "I really didn't want all this change,
and I'm sure you could use it more than I could."
Then offer the cashier ten $1 bills in exchange for a
$10 bill.

You must now get the cashier to hand over the
store's $10 bill. This can be accomplished by hold-
ing onto your money until the clerk offers you the

$10 bill. You must now take the $10 bill while simultaneously handing over the expected exchange money. What you will actually hand the cashier is nine $1 bills and a $10 bill, for a total of $19. (At this point, the clerk holds $10 that belongs to the store and nine of your dollars.)

When the cashier notices that you gave him too much, act surprised and thank him for catching the error. If he fails to catch your intentional blooper, just mention that you might have made a mistake and ask him to please recount the money.

On discovering that you gave him $19 instead of $10, tell him you just remembered your nephew's birthday and you want to give him a $20 money card. Then say, "Here, I'll add another dollar to the $19 I gave you in exchange for a $20 bill." Hand him a dollar, get your $20 and leave the store with a $10 profit. (Remember, 10 of the dollars in the cashier's hand belonged to the store, so what you actually did was to give him $10 for a $20 bill.)

Quantum physics would be easier to understand than this stuff, you protest. And at first glance, you would be correct in your assessment. All of this is difficult to grasp after only one reading, but without the confusion the scam would not work.

To gracefully mislead someone you must simultaneously carry out several activities. In the present case you made a small purchase, asked for change, made an intentional mistake, corrected it, and while making small talk cheated the store out of $10. It would, indeed, take a street-smart cashier to detect this scam in progress. Although a rare event, it can happen.

If a cashier catches you in the act, use one of the con's standard explanations:

- Apologize for the *unintentional* mistake. Act embarrassed while delivering your apology;
- Take the offensive. Use your most indignant tone of voice and point out the clerk's obvious incompetence. Also draw attention by speaking loudly. This will put the cashier on the defensive and more willing to let the matter pass without further action; or
- Play dumb. Most tellers will suspect that something is amiss, but their ignorance of the game will leave them unable to explain what they think happened.

Cover stories like these will help quash any claim that you intended to cheat the store. Lack of intent transforms a potential crime into an honest mistake.

Avoiding these problems hinges on your ability to select the most suitable cashiers. Desirable targets include those who are slow in making change and those unsure of themselves because they're new. According to professional con artists, many cashiers consider the art of making change as one of the world's greatest mysteries. Use their stupidity to your advantage and you can probably take them for everything in the register.

It's also a good idea to become an emotional chameleon. Skillful change raisers can instantly adapt themselves to any situation. They can switch in an instant from being surprised to confused, angry, or disgusted. This play-acting serves to keep the cashier off balance and eager to get them (you) out of their lives.

SHORTCHANGING

If you are an underpaid, unappreciated cashier intent on obtaining a well-deserved salary increase, shortchanging could fulfill your needs. (I should warn you that shortchanging will not work if it involves the sale of this book! Otherwise, the following routines should serve you well.)

Your customers of choice should consist of those who appear rushed and without time to count their change. When finding such a suitable sucker, leave behind a dollar or two of his change in the register, placing the receipt on top of what change you wish to return. While handing over the change, immediately inject a compliment on his hairstyle or clothing. It's sure to distract your victim and in the process make him feel good about himself. Not only will he love you for noticing how good he looks, but he might also become a regular customer. Don't kill the illusion by overacting.

If caught in the act, just apologize and give him the rest of his change. Tell him it's a bad day for you because your dog died, the kids are in the hospital, or someone just burglarized your home.

Avoid at all costs customers who appear alert and in complete control of themselves. Those who watch you enter every item into the register's memory or seem to be running a tape total in their heads do not make good victims. If you should happen to come across a change raiser while running a shortchange, please let me know how it turns out.

Here's another shortchange classic sometimes used by ticket sellers in carnival sideshows and theaters. The key to this routine involves making change as far away from the customer as possible. Slide his ticket or goods forward with one hand and his change forward with the other. While pushing the change toward him, leave some money behind under your extending arm, which comes to rest on it. Then draw your arms back, bringing the stolen money with it, and let the change fall to the cushioned floor under your feet. If caught in the act, immediately correct the problem and use the "it's a bad day" excuse.

THE ENEMY

Throughout your career as a professional con artist there will exist those intent on educating others on ways to beat you at your own game. The good news is that most who receive this knowledge either ignore it or soon forget all they have been told. Here's an example of what the cops have told cashiers over the years, with little or no effect:

If you want to beat every change raiser, regardless of his or her skill, simply remember this 100 percent guaranteed course of action: Perform only one transaction at a time.

If anyone asks for change, give it to him. Should he ask for more change before you have completed the first transaction, politely ask him to wait while you finish the first transaction. When through, close the register and take care of his second request for change. By following this simple rule, you cannot possibly lose.

Here's another example of advice ignored. This one covers till dipping.

When you give change to a till dipper, he will tip his hand slightly to let one or more coins slide off and fall to the floor behind your side of the counter. While you bend down to retrieve the coins, his fingers forage among the higher denomination bills in the open drawer of the cash register.

Several years ago in an Oklahoma City grocery, one wannabe forager tried this ploy. As the cashier stooped to pick up the fallen change she reached up and slammed the till drawer shut, breaking three fingers on the dipper's hand.

The lessons here are:

- If the cash register is within the customer's reach, clerks should never leave it open or unattended, and

- Till dippers should keep their medical insurance premiums paid.

Even though most of this crime prevention advice is ignored, there always exists the possibility of a few clerks putting this information to use. Encounter one of them, and now you know what to expect.

CHAPTER TWO

DECEPTIVE HONESTY

"You can understand lying because you practice it in a watered-down form as a daily method of smoothing the way, helping the machinery of humankind to function more easily without getting fouled by too much truth-stuff."
—Ed McBain

If you are reading this chapter from a jail's cell block for trying to run a change-raising scheme, apologies are in order. Perhaps I should have mentioned that it's best to read the entire book before venturing into the con artist's risky world. Additional chapters reveal the inherent risks associated with con artistry. If this worries you, then stay out of the business, because everything a con artist does involves risk. Without those risks you remove the challenge, the adventure, and any memorable gains. Risk serves as the essence of confidence games. The easy money, freedom, and power you will enjoy throughout your career as a professional con artist all pale in comparison to the thrill of having played the game—and having played it well. Matching wits with your prey, leading the greedy down a path of financial ruin, and avoiding capture provide a thrill reserved only for the daring and adventurous.

That you will embrace the hazards involved with your intense existence does not mean you should function as a mindless idiot. Learning how to recognize the differences between unavoidable, calculated, and foolish risks separates the professionals from the amateurs.

From here on, everything you now believe shall either be strengthened through clarification, altered, substituted, or destroyed. Your reward for enduring this attack on your beliefs consists of an ability to lead a life without confusion or limits—with all your survival instincts fiercely sharpened.

THE DEFINITION GAME

Once you abandon the notion that there exists a clear distinction between honesty and deception, you will never again understand why anyone would become a burglar, bank robber, or common thief. With so many legal ways to remain dishonest, such foolishness as armed robbery is reserved for the criminally insane. As you will discover, if dishonesty is a crime, then everyone is a criminal.

Everyone Lies

Skillfully slaughtering the truth to obtain something of value from your intended prey is called a confidence game. The outrage your conduct *should* draw from the law-abiding public has been replaced by apathy. People just don't care. Those popular "all-out war on crime" campaigns won't apply because they are reserved for crimes of violence. Although con artists cannot fully understand this, they suspect it has something to do with a common bond between themselves and their customers. Everyone lies.

You, me, and everyone else in the world tells lies. Condemning your activities as a liar requires a pretentious person willing to play the part of an honest individual. In other words, he must lie.

Subconsciously recognizing this universal inclination for lying leads to confusion and then tolerance. Being unable to separate the good people who tell lies from the evil lying criminals causes an array of deep psychological conflicts. Although you need not become a psychoanalyst to advance your career as a con artist, you had better know all there is to know about lying.

Universal Lying

Although complete honesty remains a noble idea, it is only a concept and not a reality. Certainly, there are some that are more honest than others and a few who come as close to perfection as is humanly possible. However, despite our best efforts, lying remains a universal human characteristic.

In giving you some examples of the various forms of lying, I will begin with those we all commit (which, for some, are believed to benefit society) and go on to those that can inflict various degrees of harm to others.

Etiquette Lies

"I'm pleased to meet you," "Pardon me," "You're welcome," "How are you?" "Have a nice day." We go through the day making polite utterances we often don't mean. In other words, lying with smiles on our faces. When you ask someone how he is, you don't really want to learn that his spouse just left him, the IRS is auditing his tax return, he was fired yesterday, and his car isn't functioning properly.

Technically these banal utterances are called "phatic" communication. They establish social contact rather than communicate ideas. Without them, social relationships would not flow as smoothly as they do. We can all be thankful for etiquette lies, realizing that when we commit them we are helping society.

Little White Lies

Little white lies are more lies that are socially beneficial and are used to avoid hurt feelings and maintain relationships. When we tell an etiquette lie, it is most often an unplanned, automatic utterance. In contrast, little white lies are usually anticipated and planned well ahead of situations in which we must politely avoid irritating or angering people we don't wish to alienate.

Little white lies occur so often we view them more as excuses than the untruthful statements they are. Although not as common as etiquette lies, nearly all of us tell little white lies. Given the nature of social relationships, we are virtually forced to tell them or get a reputation for being mean, stingy, crude, unfriendly, and in general, old grouches. Consider the following letter sent to a friend of mine who writes a small-town advice column:

DEAR HANK: I sure could use your help. My neighbor is constantly borrowing my tools, but I really don't want to lend them to him. He's a good neighbor and I don't know how to refuse him without hurting his feelings. What should I do?
—TROUBLED

DEAR TROUBLED: Tell him the truth. Just say you don't like lending out your tools. Although this will most likely put a slight crimp in your friendship, after he buys his own tools and finds out how expensive they are, he'll get over it.

Some little white lies are so common that they have become fodder for stand-up comic routines, eliciting laughter because everyone recognizes them for what they are. "Not tonight, dear, I have a headache" and "The check is in the mail" are prime examples.

Were they not so addictive, little white lies could certainly be deemed petty beyond belief. After all, does the harm they do outweigh the social benefits? But the teller of little white lies usually finds that success breeds contempt and soon telling little white lies becomes a habit. At this point, those little white lies lose their whiteness and grow in size to become outright lies.

If you don't recognize etiquette lies as often being falsehoods and your conscience really complains when you tell little white lies, the likelihood of your becoming a successful con artist is, frankly, remote. Fortunately, the vast majority of us are still qualified. How you handle outright lies may be the determining factor if you aspire to an easy, remunerative life playing confidence games.

Outright Lies

When we graduate from little white lies to outright lies we cross the Rubicon into the realm of falsehoods where we cannot rationalize away our lies as being harmless bits of misinformation told to simplify life. For the most part, outright lies are exploitations and we know that they are when we tell them.

If you wish to become an accomplished con artist, realize that outright lies are not and must not be bold-faced lies. Bold-faced lies arrive with blaring bugles and a roll of drums announcing their falseness as they spill over your lips. They so destroy credulity that few, if any, would accept them at face value. Effective lies must be clothed in verbal attire that gives them credence.

The con man who knocks on your door and tells you he has just finished dressing a driveway in the next block, has some sealant left over, and can consequently dress your driveway at a reduced price has masked his con in a series of outright but believable lies. Should he offer to dress your driveway with the best sealant available at less than half the price of his competitors, you would, hopefully, seriously doubt the veracity of his offer. His bold-faced lie is far too obviously a falsehood.

Lies of Omission

We may often lie as effectively by saying nothing as by speaking. Lies of omission involve the use of facts—but not all the facts. If the listener wants to assume he is being told all he needs to know, why disillusion him?

If I ask for your help because I have been forced into bankruptcy, as a friend you might well consider lending a helping hand. But add to my tale of woe that the bankruptcy came because I lost all my money at a roulette table in Las Vegas and your benevolence might cease to exist.

Con artists love lies of omission. Someone offers to trim your trees at $10 each. The price is appealing and you accept. When he finishes you discover he meant $10 for each branch, not each tree. Reread the offer and you'll realize he never specified what "each" meant.

Exaggeration Lies (Whoppers)

The real experts at exaggeration lies are fisherfolk; they commonly exaggerate sufficiently to become bold-faced liars—but then everyone expects it of them. Actually, most of us use exaggeration lies. What parent, remonstrating with a child, hasn't said, "If I've told you once, I've told you a million times. . ." When your boss says "I need a minute of your time to help me with something," you know that the "minute" could well stretch out to three minutes, three hours, or even three days. Con artists employ exaggeration lies regularly, minimizing the cost to the mark (victim) and maximizing the obvious benefits.

Unlike habitual liars, you must be stingy with your lies, using them with calculated economy and guided always by the quest for gain. Telling the truth whenever possible makes your lies more effective.

HYPOCRISY

Although your activities as a con artist parallel those of some major business institutions and governmental agencies, don't always expect equal treatment if caught. You risk being classified as a thief, a swindler, or a cheat. The activities of your competition will be called something far less damning. They will have involved themselves in unfair or misleading business practices, not thefts. To prove how fine the line is between honest and dishonest business practices let's look at a few examples.

Dialing For Dollars

You have just received a telephone call. The caller says she is a member of your local law enforcement agency. She goes on to say they are raising the funds necessary to buy bulletproof vests for all the agency's officers. She then seeks a donation from you, promising a token gift for your generosity and support.

You donate $10 and receive a note of thanks and the promised decal, plastic coffee cup, or other inexpensive gift. Assuming the caller actually represented your local law enforcement agency and the agency received money, were you just swindled or was this a legitimate business transaction?

If you classified this as a legitimate transaction, you are correct. These fund-raising activities occur every day and result in millions of dollars of donations to countless organizations.

Now let's examine what you and millions of others

don't know about some of these legitimate business practices. The knowledge you gain might cause you to alter your perspective.

The person in our real-life example is not a law enforcement officer. She is an employee of a professional fund-raising company. Of the money collected by this company, no more than 20 percent will ever reach the law enforcement agency. That's right, 80 percent or more of the donations are kept by the fund-raiser to cover expenses and, of course, turn a profit. Now that you have just donated eight of your $10 to a fund-raising company, do you still believe you were not somehow deceived?

What some of these fund-raisers have resorted to involves the use of omission lies. They omit any facts that would cause you to bypass them. Should that occur, and you donate directly to the agency, the fund-raiser would not make any money.

In comparison, let's look at another situation involving similar activities.

Illegal Donations

One day, you suddenly decide to help a needy organization. Perhaps it's a shelter for the homeless. You don't have much money of your own, so you become a one-person fund-raising organization.

You draft, print, and mail out hundreds of fund-raising letters. You also make hundreds of telephone calls seeking donations from local citizens and tell them you represent the shelter for the homeless. In all, you net over $50,000. Of that $50,000, you give the shelter for the homeless $25,000. The shelter thanks you for your donation, and a week later you are arrested and charged with theft by fraud. Why? Because it's the law.

Even though you donated a greater percentage of the money than did the *honest* fund-raising organization cited in the previous example, you were not hired by the shelter and probably didn't mention to them how the money had been raised.

In both examples, lies of one form or another were used to deceive others for personal gain. Some good also stemmed from both fund-raising activities because the officers got the bulletproof vests and the homeless received some needed clothing, food, and shelter. It might be said that no one was really harmed.

Another, less noted, difference between these two examples is that the honest business was incorporated, filed all the necessary legal papers, and worked out of an office. They also kept records and paid the requisite taxes. What professional con artists are fast learning, and so should you, is that fraud is much easier to commit when cloaked under the guise of being an honest business. In other words, learn to use the law and its inherent loopholes to your advantage.

The Truth Be Told

Amid all the dishonesty in our world, let it be known that con artists are among the most honest. Here's why.

Although con artists do indeed deceive others for personal gain, most of them make no real pretension about what they do for a living. Granted, they are masters of rationalization, but it's only because it's part of the game. In the end, almost all of them readily admit that their chosen profession is anything but honest.

This was best summed up by Yellow Kid Weil, considered to be one of the most proficient con artists of his time. In his autobiography, *The Con Game and "Yellow Kid" Weil*, as told to W.T. Brannon, he said, "I am now seventy years old and I look back over my career with mingled feelings. I have retired and I want to do what I can to promote harmony among my fellow man. For this reason, I decided to tell the inside story of my long, and I must admit, dishonorable career."

Of all the white-collar criminals I have arrested over the years, I cannot recall any of them admitting that what they did was a crime. Like con artists, they were masters at rationalizing their activities. Unlike con artists, they did not view their activities as anything more than getting caught at something everyone else is doing. And what they believe everyone else is doing is simply helping themselves to the "fringe benefits" that are ripe for the picking.

Limited Confusion

In our hearts we know that we tell lies. We forgive ourselves for this weakness because we allow ourselves to believe it is required to establish and maintain amicable social relationships. And because we forgive ourselves we are willing to forgive the little white lies and even some outright lies told by others, including those told by some business people.

This forgiveness, however, has its limits. We usually draw the line at lies that continually affect our pocketbooks or cause us physical harm. Doctors, lawyers, judges, and law officers aren't supposed to lie, and neither are others who provide us with the things we depend on.

So steadfast are we in protecting ourselves from these latter liars that we've created consumer watch groups, product safety agencies, review boards, and an army of other such lie detectors. When these safeguards fail us, we call in the lawyers and earn our reputation for being the most litigious people on the planet Earth.

Knowing how others may judge your activities, you must now put this knowledge to good use. To accomplish this, carefully monitor the present mood of those you hope to deceive. When sufficient numbers of them become angered over your activities, it's time for you to take a long vacation. When they retreat to their usual state of mass confusion and cannot tell the difference between the players and the spectators, it's time to ply your trade again.

Ignore this advice and you are playing a game you cannot possible win. Apply your talents when the public is angry and you run the risk of causing permanent and lasting damage to your profession. Using a worst-case scenario, you run the risk of becoming the catalyst for the resurrection of mass honesty.

CHAPTER THREE

MIND GAMES

"Con guys have a tendency to stick together. There's a lot of money in the games. You make a damned good living and you don't work very hard. So I went into it and I made a damned good living and I didn't work very hard."
—Frank W. Abagnale Jr.

To function as a skilled con artist, you must constantly entertain outsiders with an astounding array of well-rehearsed and believable rationalizations. Your ability to rationalize exists as an invaluable skill, second only to your proficiency in the art of bluffing. When used properly, these skills enable you to accomplish all sorts of spectacular feats, one of the most wondrous of these being the ability to get out of doing any physical labor.

Even though you have used rationalization techniques throughout your life, achieving the degree of proficiency needed to operate as a true professional requires many years of painstaking practice. Confusing your ability to deceive yourself with being able to deceive others is one way amateurs make themselves known. For example, when caught in the act of doing something wrong, an amateur says, "It's not my fault." A professional says, "Even though I acted on advice from people I trusted, advice I've since discovered to be wrong, I nevertheless accept full responsibility for my actions." In this fashion, they accept and reject the blame all in one breath.

Let's look at some other examples of how con artists color their world, and at the kinds of evidence they offer in support of their views.

HARD WORK IS FOR SUCKERS

Several years ago I had occasion to engage the husband of a Gypsy fortune-teller in a philosophical discussion involving the nature of his wife's inherently dishonest career.[1] "Why do you continue to take advantage of other people's misery and ignorance?" I asked. "Doesn't running from the law ever wear you out?"

"You must be kidding," he said. "Look at what I've got. I buy a new car every year, my wife brings in over $500,000 a year without any real effort, and I don't pay any taxes." Now well into the gloating stage he continued: "I never had to work a day in my life. Suddenly you come along and suggest that I give it up. For what? I should work like those other suckers, give half my income to the government, and be happy with a lot less? You've got to be kidding," he repeated.

"Sure," I said, "you're beating the system, but times have changed, and you and your wife will eventually have to answer for your crimes. And I think you know it."

"We're willing to take that chance," he replied. "It's what we do for a living, and we won't stop until someone stops us. And I don't see that happening any time soon."

"If I didn't know better," I said, "it appears you just fell prey to one of your wife's fanciful predictions."

He smiled, shook his head, and said, "You just keep up the hard work, Dennis, because I don't have the time for it. I've a new car to buy."

This was not my first exposure to an ideology so firmly rooted in the belief that hard work is only for suckers. On the contrary, I have never met a con artist who believed otherwise. Another version of this rationalization came from a career con artist I arrested for posing as a police officer. In defending his choice of professions, he offered the following: "The only jobs I could get before becoming a con man were always low-paying, go-nowhere jobs. Now I make a lot of money. I get to travel all over the country, and I don't have to answer to nobody." He closed with, "I'm doing what hardworking suckers would like to be doing, but they just don't have the guts to take a chance."

Moral of the story: Why work when there's an easier way?

GENTLE PERSUASION

As a professional con artist, you must maintain an unwavering commitment to never hurting anyone. *Hurt* is murder, armed robbery, rape, and any other of those hideous crimes of violence. In contrast, confidence games exist as an art where one uses words to persuade others to hand over their money. As the pros see it, con games are simply minor infractions of the law, unworthy of any serious attention. What's more, they aren't the only ones faithful to this belief.

In January 1994, I was interviewed by a radio talk show host from California. What began as an inquisitive probing about the contents of a book that Dr. John Dowling and I had written about Gypsy-perfected frauds soon turned into an inquisition. Why, the host demanded, was I was so obsessive in my beliefs about fraud?

With no intention of allowing me to respond, he quickly pointed out that our nation was experiencing a major crime wave. "Citizens are being murdered in their homes, and other crimes of violence are on the increase!" he exclaimed.

Then, speaking to his audience he said, "I think most of you would join with me in asking our nation's police officers to stop wasting their time chasing petty thieves, and to concentrate their efforts on combating real crimes."

Were it not for a convenient commercial break, followed by the end of the program, I would have responded with two brief statements. The first would be a correction. Violent crimes involving average citizens are not on the increase. What has increased is the sensationalized media coverage on violent crime. Why this occurs will be discussed in Chapter Eight.

The second comment would have been to thank the host on behalf of our nation's "petty thieves" and con artists. If they were listening, I have no doubt that they were appreciative of his effort to reinforce what they have been saying all along: Without an act of violence, there is no crime.

JUST REWARDS

Put these words to memory: THE SUCKERS GET WHAT THEY DESERVE. These six words accurately describe every victim of every fraud that has been, or ever will be, committed. Here's why.

Assuming your potential customers each possess the ability to make rational choices, they are willing participants and not victims. If you decide to buy a stolen car and that car suddenly breaks down, calling yourself a victim might make you feel better, but you would be wise to keep such complaints to yourself.

The same principle applies to fraud. If I ask you to join me in fleecing someone else, and in the end it is you who gets taken, then you're not a victim. To the contrary, you just got what you deserved.

As Yellow Kid Weil put it: "The men I swindled were

motivated by a desire to acquire money, and they didn't care at whose expense they got it. . . . I took money only from those who could afford it and were willing to go in with me in schemes they fancied would fleece others."

Impostor, con man, and master forger Frank Abagnale took a slightly different view and believed anyone stupid enough to invest blind faith in him deserved to be swindled. In this view, a sucker is anyone possessing a willingness to accept someone at face value.

Before examining other rationalizations, let's look into a con game that shows why suckers get what they deserve. This particular game, known as three-card monte, is a relative of the shell game. The first important fact, here, is that both games are without a doubt the most exposed scams in the history of fraud. Television, radio, magazines, newspapers, and many books have repeatedly made it clear that three-card monte and the shell game are not games. That is, of course, unless you consider it a game to play something where you have no chance of winning—absolutely none!

The only props needed are three playing cards, usually two black spot cards and a red queen. You toss the cards face down, moving them from one place to another.

The sucker must locate the queen. After several successful guesses show him how easy it is to win, the sucker places a cash bet. Once the money is on the table, you (after many hours of practice) manipulate the cards so that the queen is never where the sucker thinks it is. There are many ways to do this.

For one, intentionally crimp or bend the upper corner on the queen. After letting the chump believe you have blundered, remove the bend from the queen and bend one of the spot cards while throwing them down on the table (bar, packing crate, whatever). Because of the plastic coating on the cards, this sleight-of-hand bending will not leave any telltale signs.

Another method involves holding the three cards, one on top of the other, in one hand. Leave a space between each of the cards so the spacing is visible to the sucker. Let the sucker see that the top card in your hand is the queen. As you toss the cards, make it appear you are throwing the top card, the queen. What you will throw is the center card. After some practice, this move is completely undetectable, even if done in slow motion. To stress the obvious, it's important to know where you tossed the queen. Should your sleight of hand get out of hand, your next trick should include a disappearing act.

Get serious! you say, this could only work on the brain-dead. Though hard to believe, three-card monte was invented more than 100 years ago and has changed little in the intervening decades. It worked then and continues to work thousands of times every day. If you want to invest the hours needed to become a skillful "broad tosser" (three-card monte dealer) there are no better instructions than those in S.W. Erdnase's *The Expert at the Card Table*, first published in 1902 and republished many times since.

NOBODY CARES

How serious is fraud? What is being done to curtail fraudulent activities? Before you answer, here's how a con artist with more than 53 arrests for fraud answered these questions.

"I'm no genius, and the scams I run are not complicated. If anyone was serious about putting an end to my career, it could be done easily and swiftly. But I'm still in business." He went on to say the average punishment for his many crimes consisted of meager fines or restitution, which is nothing more than giving back what he had taken. In all, his profits far outweighed the modest risk of receiving any serious punishment.

From a practical vantage point, this is not so much a con artist's attempt at rationalization as an unpleasant fact. As author David Mauer once remarked: "The public tends to regard theft from the person, however cleverly executed, as comical; it's a trick, like the one performed by a magician."

When it comes down to it, about the only people really concerned about fraud are the suckers who get fleeced. And even their concern isn't that impressive. If it were otherwise, then why do crime surveys suggest that only one out of every 10 fraud victims ever reports his victimization to the police? Is it because the other nine realized they got what they deserved? Or, could it be that no one cares? Con artists don't care; either view serves them well.

EVERYBODY DOES IT

From a con's perspective, the thin line that once separated his activities from legitimate business practices now exists in theory only. Doing Unto Others Before They Do Unto You has become a commonplace occurrence.

As author Robert Pinckert once noted, "(L)awyers lie and win cases, politicians lie and win elections, advertisers lie and make bags of money, parents lie to children, and the sexes lie to one another." In other words, lying (which makes deception possible) is an everyday event and no longer shocks our senses.

In Chapter Two, we talked about our tendency toward classifying, rather than rejecting, lies. Within these classifications are two major categories: lies we are willing to live with, and those we reject. The deceptions used by con artists have been classified as unacceptable. After all, they're strangers and they don't provide any useful services. What's more—they're criminals.

Unlike us, professional con artists waste no time equivocating. For them, their activities are nothing more than a polished duplication of what everyone else is doing.

Over the years, various con artists have provided an abundance of examples of how business people scam their customers. While you read the following selections, keep in mind that *deception,* as used here, means any intentional or unscrupulous lie or tactic used to obtain, or to attempt to obtain, money from others.

Bait Scam

Your neighborhood TV and appliance store advertises a television with a price far below that of any of their competitors. Because you have only five shopping days left until Christmas, you decide that this would make a great gift for a special relative. You appear at the store and express your desire to buy the advertised TV. The salesperson immediately lowers his voice and asks if you're sure you want to invest your money in this set.

Being curious, you ask him what he means. He tells you the only reason the televisions are on sale is because the boss wants to get rid of them. He goes on to say that a new shipment of better quality TVs, loaded with extras not available on the advertised set, has just arrived. For just an extra $100 you can give your beloved relative a TV that will last for many years to come.

When, and only when, you insist on buying the advertised set, will the salesperson give up the game. Then, too, he might claim the sets are out of stock and issue a rain check. Any back orders will, of course, take several weeks to fill—well past Christmas.

What is at work during these games are store owners willing to bet that with some pressure they can sell you a more expensive item. They also know there are plenty of people who are just too dumb to take advantage of the bargain item.

The bait scam is similar to what you might know as bait and switch. However, in the bait and switch you have no chance of getting the sale item. Either the item doesn't exist, or if it does exist, only a handful are available. To escape state laws or municipal ordinances intended to curb this type of business-perfected fraud, the sale ads need only contain these familiar words: "While supplies last." These supplies, of course, are exhausted only minutes after the store opens for business.

Another closely related scam involves stores that guarantee to beat their competitors' prices. They will also pay you the difference for any of their own merchandise that you buy that goes on sale within a specific time. This is just a gimmick using refunds and price matching as the bait. They are aware most people don't comparison shop, and neither do they have the time to invest in a daily check on sale items. In other words, they are betting that they can beat you at a game they've created, and one for which they make all the rules. They've never met my wife Donna.

A few days after buying a refrigerator at the regular price, she saw it being advertised as a sale item. On returning to the store for a price adjustment, she was surprised to find that rather than being cheaper, it was now being sold for $20 *more* than she had paid. In a matter-of-fact tone, the clerk explained that Donna had purchased the appliance on a one-day, nonadvertised special sale, not to be confused with today's regular sale. She would get no refund. But just three days later, Donna saw the store's latest advertisement listing the refrigerator for $70 less than she'd paid. With no desire to hear yet another fanciful tale from the sales clerk, Donna simply returned to the store, got her $70 adjustment, and left knowing that she had just beaten the merchants at their own game.

Marketing Scams

We know that con artists manipulate others for profit. Because they view their "customers" as nothing more than a source of income while pretending to be their friends, we at times despise them. Yet, is this any different from the treatment we often receive from advertisers?

Product advertisements are, of course, necessary, because they let us know what's available. What the product does, how it's made, and how it compares to similar products are all useful pieces of information. Not so useful are ads based on the belief that our mental capacity is somehow deficient and therefore open to any nonsense they care to present.

Take a few minutes to locate a magazine containing various product advertisements. Randomly select any ad, and then examine it closely. What you will find is an abundance of hype and a lack of useful information.

An ad of this caliber recently appeared in a major woman's magazine. Hoping to sell its hosiery, a company took out a full-page ad. Mind you, this was not just any hosiery, but state-of-the-art "body contouring" hosiery. The ad depicted an extremely healthy young woman. Beneath her picture, in large bold print, appeared the words, DON'T DO LEG LIFTS WHEN YOU CAN BUY THEM. The readers were also advised to stop killing themselves to get something that comes "naturally" with the use of this fantastic hosiery.

Did the advertisers believe any intelligent woman with heavy legs would think that hosiery is a substitute for exercise, or there is a "natural" way to do the unnatural? What this ad should have said was, "If you're stupid enough to think you can look like this without any effort on your part, then we have what you need."

Just like con artists, the manufacturer of this product knows what we want is seldom compatible with what is possible. But why bother being realistic when it's much easier, and far more profitable, to feed our delusions? Companies that use ads of this type know that no one would consciously believe what they've said. Subconsciously, however, plenty of people will decide that trying the product can't hurt, and who knows—it might even help a little.

Other ads promise to do things that can't possibly be verified. Skin cream manufacturers, for example, claim that daily use of their product will reduce wrinkles. But unless you use the cream and your twin sister doesn't, how can you possibly know what you would have looked like without its use?

If the product fails to meet your expectations, you have no legal recourse. Don't forget, these were your expectations, not the manufacturer's. The ad simply said the product would reduce wrinkles. What it didn't say was exactly how much. As any proficient con artist already knows, being purposely vague has its rewards.

But what about those advertisers who are specific in their claims? How could they possibly deceive us?

If you've ever attended a magic show, you already have the answer. Even when you know the magician is about to deceive you, seldom are you aware of how the deception worked. Thanks to some misdirection, ample amounts of showmanship, and lies of omission, the obvious is always overlooked.

In the same fashion, advertisers who list the specifics in their advertisements and have something to hide will do everything possible to misdirect your attention. What they want you to read and believe is always colorfully represented. The use of fine print and deceptive language is reserved for the bad news.

Petty examples? Perhaps. But at what point does a deception become a crime? Some might say there must exist an intent to deceive. Unfortunately, intent is not easy to prove. You must first know what was in the person's mind, and then be able to back your belief with solid evidence. If the person is clever enough, you will have no chance of proving his or her intent beyond a reasonable doubt.

Others might suggest that it's the amount of money involved. If so, how much money must be obtained before it becomes a crime? Is it a crime to cheat 10,000 people out of 50 cents, one person out of $5,000, both, or none of the above?

Honest-Joe Scams

There remains one other group of con artists who disguise themselves as honest, law-abiding citizens. One such citizen forced the McDonald's corporation to give her more than $2.9 million because she spilled hot coffee on herself while riding in her grandson's car. If this wasn't a scam, I would be wise to add the following warning label to this book: AUTHOR'S WARNING! EATING BOOKS CAN INDUCE CONSTIPATION, INDIGESTION, AND AIRWAY OBSTRUCTIONS.

Here's a brief list of other thefts and scams performed by this group we call honest citizens:

- Selling the family car but intentionally withholding information about the car's major defects.
- Reporting a burglary to the insurance company and then padding the list of stolen property with property that never existed.
- Taking part in pyramid schemes fully realizing that others will be cheated in the process.
- Falling prey to a con artist and then telling the police you were the victim of an armed robbery.

And the list goes on.

Do not be fooled by the amateur status of our society's semi-honest citizens. Many of them do pull off at least one good scam in their lifetimes. As a professional, you shall have greater control over your successes because you will have learned well the art of being sincere in a deceitful way. If you insist on feeling good about yourself, get a job.

1. A bit of explanation is required at this point. *License to Steal: Traveling Con Artists: Their Games, Their Rules—Your Money*, a book I wrote with John Dowling, examined the culture of Gypsies in America in depth. In it, we explained who we are talking about when we use the term "Gypsy": "Most Gypsies, or Romani, as they prefer to call themselves, have . . . joined the labor force, own homes, send their sons and daughters to college, vote, pay taxes, and serve in the armed forces. But there is a substantial segment of the Romani population that has not assimilated and shows no inclination to do so. In fact, these latter Romani heartily reject, despise, and condemn American society. . . . We are not casting any aspersions on the majority of Romani . . . when we speak of Gypsy crime. What we are trying to do is focus attention on that element of Romani society that, through its criminal activities, creates a negative image for all Romani. . ."

CHAPTER FOUR

TOOLS OF THE TRADE

Truman's Law—If you can't convince them, confuse them.
—Harry S. Truman[1]

A professional con artist plays a variety of roles that change with the game. He may play the part of rancorous cynic or affable romantic, blue-blooded sophisticate or rustic commoner. But whatever he may seem, he is proficient in his ability to inspire faith and confidence in those with whom he deals and misdeals.

Proving the obvious is often overlooked, the significant role that *confidence* plays in all scams escaped public notice until 1849. Before that time, had you read everything written on the topic of fraud, you would have received meticulous details about the various frauds and the scoundrels who committed them. Missing from these documents was any mention of confidence, con artists, or confidence crimes. The great mystery of the era was not *how* the scams worked—but *why* they worked.

When, eventually, you did discover the vital link between swindles, frauds, and confidence, you would have been reading the July 8, 1849, edition of the *New York Herald*. It was on that date they reported the arrest of a swindler using the name Wm. Thompson.

On July 7, Thompson was arrested in New York on the complaint of a Mr. Thomas McDonald. McDonald claimed that Thompson had tricked him out of his gold watch. The *Herald* described the incident in this way:

> Arrest of the Confidence Man—For the last few months a man has been traveling about the city, known as the "Confidence Man": that is, he would go up to a perfect stranger in the street, and being a man of genteel appearance, would easily command an interview. Upon this interview he would say, after some little conversation, "have you confidence in me to trust me with your watch until to-morrow"; the stranger, at this novel request, supposing him to be some old acquaintance, not at the moment recollected, allows him to take the watch, thus placing "confidence" in the honesty of the stranger, who walks off laughing, and the other, supposing it to be a joke, allows him so to do. . .[2]

Because the *New York Herald* and Thompson assisted in transforming *swindles* into *confidence crimes*, does not mean Thompson was the first swindler, thief, hustler, or scoundrel to gain the confidence of his intended mark. Every con artist that has ever lived had to gain the mark's confidence during the scam. This is not an option—it's a must. (A *mark*, as used by the cons, means a victim or intended victim.)

TOOLS OF THE TRADE

In gaining a mark's confidence you will play more roles

than a Hollywood actor. You will combine the talents of a magician, a psychologist, a detective, a politician, a lawyer, a storyteller, or whatever else it takes to transform you into a person with extraordinary powers of persuasion. But the ability to act is not the only talent you must foster. You will need to develop many skills and address many concerns before taking your act to your targets.

Role-Playing

Role-playing is something you do every day. Do you not, for instance, act differently at home than you do at work? Your behavior at a party is not the same as it is when attending a funeral or an awards ceremony.

Role-playing is so common that in the early 1960s, noted psychiatrist Dr. Eric Berne wrote two books on the subject: *Games People Play* and *What Do You Say After You Say Hello*? Having read both books, and having spoken with hundreds of con artists, the only observable difference I saw between us and con artists is our choice of roles, or as Berne labeled them, "games."

What role you play depends on the selected mark. Although each mark possesses unique characteristics and weaknesses, they also share many similarities. In the next chapter we will look at the differences, but for now here's a handy reference list of the most commonly shared human weaknesses:

- Millions of Americans dream of a path to easy riches. With your help, their dreams can appear to come true.
- Compared with con artists, the average citizen leads a drab, humdrum, and unglamorous life and is willing to seize any opportunity that promises some excitement. This is where your talents as an entertainer and storyteller come in handy. If your deal

appears believable and exciting and can stir their innermost emotions, then they will do and believe almost anything.

- If given a choice, people will always believe what is comfortable to believe. They don't like difficult problems, confusion, or pain. They so desperately want to escape from reality that regardless of how outrageous your scheme might be, they will seize the bait if it promises them the comfort they seek.
- Everyone you meet will be *able* to think. Luckily for you, most of them won't. Thinking is just too damned difficult, time-consuming, and best left to the intellectuals. After allowing you to do their thinking, the possibilities for exploitation are endless.
- Somewhere within everyone lurks a demon named Greed. Reach that demon and you will indeed become the game master.

Having selected your potential mark you must now find out what game he is most willing to play.

Doing Your Homework

Contrary to popular belief, a mark is not a person who just happened to be in the wrong place at the wrong time. This belief suggests that the cons simply pick their marks at random. Those prone to making such selections usually consist of the feebleminded or those seeking a warm jail cell during the icy days of winter.

In sizing up the intended mark, the more you know about that person the greater your chances for success. The depth and scope of the information needed depends on the scam. The general rule here is the more complicated the scam, the more information you will need about the mark, his business, and his bank accounts.

The chart on the next page will provide you with examples of the types of information needed for any particular con game. Designed with ease of use in mind, I have purposely avoided listing the many classifications said to exist between the *short con* and the *big con*. I do this only because the cons couldn't care less about what the scam is called. For them, if

GAMES INVOLVED	SHORT CONS	KNOWLEDGE REQUIRED
• Most Street Games • Block Hustle • Three-Card Monte • Lost Pet Scam • Bogus Charity Schemes (door-to-door solicitations) • Change Raising	Those games where the mark is taken for the money on their person, and the con's contact with the mark is brief. 	• Best location to locate marks, i.e., shopping malls, bus or train stations, parking lots, etc. • Class of marks most apt to fall for the scheme. • Number of other cons working the area. • Best time of day to run scam. • Has local news media recently alerted citizens about your particular scam?

	BIG CONS	
• Bank Examiner • Pigeon Drop • Lottery Scam • Badge-Play Comeback • Jamaican Switch • Fortune Telling • Investment Schemes • Business Frauds (Tool restoration, advertisement & billing schemes, building repair scams.)	Those games where con has repeated or extended contact with the mark. Mark must obtain money from home or their financial institution. Usual take is $5,000 and up. 	• Size of mark's bank account. • Likelihood of interference from mark's family, friends, and neighbors. • Class of mark most apt to fall for particular scam. • Amount of time needed to delay mark's discovery of the scam. • Amount of time needed to safely flee the area. • Method most apt to prevent mark from reporting the scam to the police. • Mark's occupation, level of education, hobbies and interests.

it works, it's a good con. If it doesn't, then it isn't a con at all, but just another way not to hustle someone.

Partners In Crime

Running a scam solo is not always possible. There are times when you will have to work with one or more accomplices. Here enters a serious potential problem.

Never, but never, allow yourself to believe that you can trust an accomplice: They will turn on you in an instant. If there is any chance to cut a deal with the cops they'll seize the opportunity, because deals equal reduced or no jail time. Cons might stick together, but when their personal freedom is at stake this camaraderie quickly dissipates. It's true, there is no honor among thieves.

Knowing this, you must retain complete control. Above all else, tell those with whom you must work only what they need to know. Never supply them with your true name, or anything else that might lead to your capture. Remember what was said earlier—there are always risks involved. Your job is to minimize those risks. Being paranoid is necessary, and to misuse a familiar advertising jingle—Don't leave home without it.

Being Ordinary In An Amazing Way

At this point, you have selected your mark and conducted your research. The next step is to choose a suitable role. Depending on your choice of games, that role might include playing the part of an idiot, a business executive, a foreign citizen, a police officer, bank examiner, and so on. If you can't decide what role to play, then you won't know how to act, how to speak, how to dress, or whether you need to blend in or stand out.

Let's use the change-raising routine outlined in Chapter One as an example. First, would you want to stand out and draw attention, or might it be a wiser to blend in the with the other patrons? Second, if the clerk becomes suspicious and begins to resist, should you become aggressive or passive?

The correct answers, in order, are *blend in*, and *it depends*. The difficult question is how to cope with a suspicious clerk.

With experience you'll develop a knack for knowing when to attack and when to back off. If your mark, in this instance the clerk, becomes suspicious, then any aggressiveness will worsen the situation. Under such circumstances, your wisest choice would be an immediate departure. If the mark appears confused, the proper course of action is aggressiveness.

Before moving on, here's one other item you need to know. Like professional actors, con artists are not endowed with equal abilities. When an actor isn't right for the part, it ends with a bad review. With con artists, this mismatch ends in jail. All of which means, if you stink, give up the role and select one you're good at.

How To Talk Without Saying Anything

Without an ability to use words effectively, your chances of becoming a professional con artist don't exist. Trying to run a successful con game without an ability to confuse, convince, or impress others will guarantee you a one-way ticket to prison. Now that you've been properly cautioned, let's examine a few of the verbal tools every good con artist must have.

Rhetorical Wonders

Your most useful tool is an ability to talk a lot without saying anything. Politicians have mastered this technique and depend on it for their survival. Knowing this, you now own the solution to a real mystery. No longer will you be perplexed when the news media invests an hour or more trying to explain what a politician just said during a five-minute remark. In reality, they are just as confused as you are, so they cover every conceivable possibility.

So, you ask, exactly how does one go about saying nothing with words? In essence, evasive communication requires a total commitment to the use of balanced reciprocal communication techniques that have proven time and time again to be extremely effective in all conceivable linguistic interactions. STOP! Read the last sentence again, and this time try to comprehend what was said.

Still confused? I hope so. If you gained any useful information from what you have just read, it was an accident, because I didn't say anything. By using abstract and otherwise equivocal and meaningless rhetoric, it's easy to manipulate your intended audience. Con artists use it to control their marks, knowing that people do indeed believe what they least understand.

Being curious, I have on several occasions experimented with the use of obfuscation. During my public presentations on fraud, I would suddenly interject such phrases as functional logistical programming, raised associative sensitivity, fraudulent centric paradigms, and so on.

Immediately following this confusion, I would pause and ask the audience if they had any questions. Their silence was the only response. After disclosing the experiment, each admitted that because I was serious and appeared knowledgeable, they simply assumed they were the only ones in the audience who didn't understand what was said. Any questions were thought to be a public display of their ignorance.

Believe me, this nonsense works. College professors use it to keep students in line, politicians use it to avoid accountability, police officers use it to obtain confessions, lawyers use it because they acquired it from the college professors in law school, and the list goes on. Learning that professional con artists also use it is no great revelation.

Just because my examples made use of some rather hefty multisyllabic words—such as multisyllabic—does not mean that smaller and more familiar words won't have the same effect. Here are a few examples I've borrowed from con artists and a few others:

This is a con artist trying to sell a cheap imitation gold necklace: "I am completely confident that you will be totally satisfied with this necklace." (Purposely missing from this is any mention of why the customer will be satisfied and what will be done for those who are dissatisfied.)

Here's an arrested con artist responding to a police officer who just asked him for his home address: "I used to live in Chicago, but I recently moved to Milwaukee to live with my aunt. But, as luck would have it, she got sick and is now in a nursing home, so I had to move out. Could I bum a cigarette off you?" (Try listing that address in a report.)

This is an amateur con artist telling a judge why he conned several senior citizens out of their life savings: "Your honor, I thank you for allowing me the opportunity to explain my actions. I really have a lot of problems with my family lately. When I came to Milwaukee, I thought that I could get my life turned around, but I was obviously mistaken. Any leniency you might extend to me will certainly be greatly appreciated. And again, thank you for allowing me to have some say in all of this." (With this fact-filled—albeit nonresponsive—explanation, the judge handed down a nine-year jail sentence.)

Just for the fun of it, this is a politician talking to her constituents: "With resolute determination I will restore law and order in our community." (This is indeed an indistinct plan that will definitely achieve nothing that she could be held accountable for.)

Finally, here's a classic used by most parents when trying to discipline their children and still leave their options open: "You better behave—or else!"

Pure Manipulation

By now you should have a basic understanding of what is needed before approaching your intended mark. It took a while to get to this point, but the payoff is near. Having approached the mark you will now focus on gaining his or her confidence.

Unlike a doctor, whose position fosters trust and confidence, you are a stranger. Any trust or confidence you seek must be obtained through trickery.

Let's devise a list of those qualities that go into the making of the people we trust. Picture in your mind those people whom you most trust and admire. Do not include family members on this list. Now ask yourself how these people look, act, and speak. When finished, review your list and see if there are any similarities among these people.

Here's the list I came up with:

Confident: They know what they're doing (or so it appears).

Humorous: They have a good sense of humor and often make fun of themselves. Never do they joke at the expense of others.

Sincere: They appear interested in other's problems and are eager to lend a helping hand whenever possible.

Knowledgeable: They possess a great amount of knowledge about a wide variety of topics.

Calm: They never panic. The worse the impending crisis, the calmer they become.

Gracious: They do not flaunt themselves and are not pretentious. They never talk down to anyone, and they make you feel that they're glad to be in your presence.

Now who wouldn't trust a person with these qualities? Besides con artists and fraud investigators, most people would—and do—invest a great deal of faith in those who do and say all the right things at the right times.

I have excluded cons artists and fraud investigators from this list of trusting souls only because their experience tells them that some people are just too slick, too perfect, or too charming to be believed. This is a good point to keep in mind when faking any of the attributes of an honorable person. Play your role, but don't overdo it.

Turnaround Confidence

Under most circumstances, it is the con artist who must seek the confidence of the mark. But as you are about to see, there are times when it is the mark who seems to have to prove his trustworthiness to gain the confidence of the con artist.

The names and mechanics of these types of scams vary. However, the underlying premise remains constant. In each, you use your acting abilities to convince the intended mark that you're a moron, naive, or both. You also make it known that you hold a large sum of cash.

With your tale (the story you want the mark to accept), lead them to believe you either have no need for the money or can't keep it. The most common story, known as the *Jamaican Switch*, involves an inheritance from a dearly departed American relative. Being from a foreign country that forbids its citizens from bringing in more than $1,000 in U.S currency, you just don't know what to do with the rest of the inheritance. (Remember, you're an idiot, so you haven't given the idea of a currency exchange any thought.)

At this point, you have a bright idea about what to do with the money. Perhaps the person you are speaking with would be so kind as to donate the money, in your name, to a charity of his choice. For his time and trouble he would, of course, receive $500.

Continuing with your role as a moron who is now trying to make an intelligent decision, you bait the hook with something like this: "I really need your help, but how do I know I can trust you? Heck, you could keep all this money for yourself and I'd have no way of knowing. Maybe you could show me that you have enough money of your own. That way I'll know you won't be tempted to keep this here money for yourself."

After you have flashed what appears to be a large wad of money, the mark won't be hearing much of anything else you might say. He will be too busy silently contemplating how he intends to spend all the money. Not just the $500 you offered him, but all of it. The rest is child's play.

The mark goes to his bank and withdraws his money. You take the money and place it into a large handkerchief, cloth bag, or whatever else you brought along for this part of the show.

Incidentally, "your money" consists of something called a *Michigan Role*, or *Mich Role* for short. This bundle of money consists of a large denomination bill on the top and bottom of the stack, and blank paper or $1 bills between.

Having wrapped the money you now distract the mark's attention, then switch the handkerchief for one that is identical but contains nothing but scrap paper. A quick thank you followed by an equally quick departure ends the scam. The greedy victim discovers the loss, becomes emotional, and eventually continues on with his life—a lot wiser than before, but with less money.

Confidential Checklist

To ensure that you are properly equipped, carefully review the following checklist. As with any toolbox, the routine use of all the equipment is unlikely. However, when you do need a special tool, you'll always be thankful that it's there.

___ **LEGAL KNOWLEDGE**: Know the laws that apply to your chosen profession. You can't hope to evade that which you don't know exists. And remember, laws vary from state to state.

___ **BAIL MONEY**: Always have access to a sizable stash of bail money in case of an arrest. Since you have not committed a "real" crime (because you didn't harm anyone) your release is almost a certainty. Once released, leave the state as quickly as you can.

___ **IDENTIFICATION**: Always carry bogus identification. When the cops figure out your true identity you'll have already disappeared, which is another reason to have bail money available. Fake identification of all types can be obtained on the Internet, or prepared right at home using your computer and scanner.

___ **CONSISTENCY**: Never tell the truth. When caught in a lie, respond with another lie.

___ **CONTROL**: Never lose control of any situation. Planning will reduce potential errors and problems, but when they do occur, always act in a calm and calculating manner. Never lose your temper unless it's part of your role.

___ **OBSERVATION**: Always stay alert. You must have an ability to see and hear what other people overlook or ignore. Moreover, always be on the lookout for any possible setups. Should the police arrive, you must be able to spot them before they spot you.

___ **CONCENTRATION**: Always concentrate on the game. Allowing yourself to become distracted can only end with disaster. Remember, when on a road trip working the marks, you're not on vacation.

___ **WHEELS**: When running a scam, never use your own car. In most states, property used in the commission of a crime can be seized. Lease or rent a car, and always under one of your aliases. There's no sense in making it easy for the cops to trace your movements, so change cars often.

___ **POLICY**: Never use, or threaten to use, force when working a mark. Do so and you have just entered a new game with different rules and greater risks.

___ **ARTICULATION**: Using the right words to say what the mark wants to hear is a must. Always remember, what people want is seldom what they need.

___ **DETACHMENT**: Forgo all personal relationships. Close companions, family members, lovers, and friends will always betray you.

___ **RULES**: The only rules you must follow are your rules. Break those rules, and prepare to face possible arrests, convictions, and imprisonment.

1. Laurence, Peter J. Dr. *Peter's Quotations: Ideas for Our Time.* New York: Morrow, 1977.

2. Bergmann, Johannes D. "The Original Confidence Man." *American Quarterly*, Vol. XXI Fall 1969 No. 3.

CHAPTER FIVE

THE CHARACTERISTICS
OF A FOOL

*I never cease to be dumfounded by the
unbelievable things people believe.
—Leo Rosten[1]*

The truism that a fool and his money are soon parted is as valid today as it was more than 400 years ago when it became a popular saying. Thus, when you relieve fools of their money you are merely fulfilling prophecy. By targeting and playing those who possess an ability to exercise common sense and judgment, but who foolishly refrain from doing so, you victimize no one.

While real criminals create victims, con artists provide enlightenment to the uninformed. Where criminals take and give nothing in return, con artists provide a constant reminder of the losses associated with greed. But too often, instead of standing up and taking responsibility for their greed or lack of judgment and common sense, your marks will overlook their own faults and play the role of helpless victim. This status allows them to pretend they had no control over the situation.

The public treats these self-proclaimed victims with curious ambivalence. Openly they offer commiseration and sympathy, damning the culprits who would take advantage of them. Privately they think the fools probably had it coming, a perspective often shared by the police.

Fools, of course, are not a distinct, isolated category of the human race. We all devolve more or less frequently from being Homo sapiens (wise humans) to become Homo saps. Who among us has not done something impetuous or ill-advised that he or she hasn't subsequently rued? We all become fools on occasion.

In 1994, a New York judge handed down a decision that gave thousands of con artists a reason to cheer. While reviewing a case of an arrested con man, the judge declared that three-card monte was a legitimate game of chance and not a crime.

Why some people fail to grasp what should be obvious is debatable. That such failures occur is a fact. As for the con artists, the whole affair is yet another example of the foolishness that makes fraud so damned easy.

ZEROING IN

Like a shark swimming in food-infested waters, you can afford to be finicky when selecting your prey. To help you with this selection let's turn to the experts. Using the wealth of available information from our nation's con artists, and those who specialize in the study and interpretation of human behavior, I have categorized the types of fools you can expect to encounter during your career. I hasten to add that this labeling is politically incorrect, unfair, and outright vicious. But so is fraud.

Professional Pigeons
The first and the hardest to understand group of avail-

THE CHARACTERISTICS OF A FOOL

able fools are those who repeatedly fall for the same game. Even more amazing is that members of this unusual group will intentionally seek your services. Though incredibly hard to believe, some professional victims have fallen for the identical scam on as many as five different occasions.

The reasons for this phenomenon are many, but the most plausible explanation comes from the psychiatrist, Dr. Eric Berne. According to Berne, such individuals fall into the category of people who believe "you can't trust anybody." To prove their belief, they intentionally seek out those who are untrustworthy and then proclaim, "See, I told you so!"

Though easy to dupe, this particular group also has the distinction of being among the most self-righteous and vindictive. Running a game with such people requires special care. They will quickly report their encounter to the police, the news media, their state senators, the president, or anyone else who will listen to them. And they will persist until the evil villain who so wronged them is captured and put to death. Lesson learned: Never underestimate your mark's ability to do you harm.

The Old Folks

The second most dangerous group is the elderly. They are dangerous not because they are aggressive, vindictive, or mean-spirited, but because they own an image. With millions of baby boomers holding fast to the mental vision of poor, defenseless grandma and grandpa sitting in their favorite rockers idling away their remaining time, you'd best use caution. Although this stereotypical image of older adults is outdated and consequently angers them, it has gained a life of its own and will not die a natural death any time soon. The reason for its longevity is that it is appealing to many who have not yet achieved the requisite age.

The news media thrive on such stereotypical images and keep the myth alive. Politicians, aware that older adults represent a sizable voting bloc, never take lightly any negative activity directed at these people. Legislators follow suit and convert actions that would be misdemeanors if perpetrated against a younger person into felonies when used against a senior citizen. Many police officers, doctors, nurses, and others who work with the elderly when they are most sick, most senile, and most dependent, wrongfully assume that all who are old suffer the same frailties.

What almost everyone—except con artists—has failed to notice is that this group of people holds most of the nation's wealth. They own most of the available real estate, are living longer and healthier lives than at any other time in history, and are anything but senile and defenseless. Con artists are also aware that these people are just as greedy, just as foolish, and just as willing to play the game as anyone else. The only real problem involved in working older marks is, once again, in the selection.

Great effort must be made to avoid that small percentage of older adults whom the aging process has not treated fairly, that is, those who are frail and feeble. Though tempting, most professional con artists are satisfied with leaving the eradication of such wealth to the experts—such as the immediate family or dishonest health-care providers.

Older adults are especially susceptible to bank-examiner frauds, pigeon drops, investment swindles, sweetheart schemes, and contest-winner scams. Why?

One reason is that they are more trusting. Growing up in an era where most people could be trusted is something that remains with them, and it is a habit hard to break. It is a trait used to the advantage of many con artists, but mainly by those pulling the bank-examiner con.

As Alphonse Mortier, once considered to be the epitome of the bank-examiner cons in the Midwest, told me, "You wouldn't believe what these people will tell a stranger over the telephone." He says they provided him with their bank-account numbers, exact balances, and many other details about their personal lives. All of which he used to significantly reduce the amount of money they had to worry about.

Many elderly people are lonely and eager for companionship. They will spend hours on the telephone, even carrying on lengthy conversations with people who call them by mistake. It was just such a "wrong-number" strategy that Mortier used to elicit information from those he swindled. Lonely widows and widowers will frequently strike up conversations with strangers they meet in the library, coffee shops, ice-cream parlors, and so on. They are consequently ripe for sweetheart scams. That is, if the con artist can get the potential mark involved in a romantic relationship, he or she can usually siphon off a considerable amount of the available wealth. The women of one notorious crime family even married their marks and slowly poisoned them.

Another reason some older adults become easy prey is because they are often bored and looking for some excitement—not the skydiving or mountain-climbing type of excitement, but intellectually challenging excitement. Topping this list are investment opportunities. Once again, it's not the money they're after, it's the challenge. And there is no shortage of con artists who are capable of providing them with all the challenging adventures they can possibly handle.

Greed is also an important factor. "Offer them a chance to cash-in on a lucrative but shady deal and they'll beat a path to your door," claimed one con artist. Other cons have noted that their older clients had more money than they could spend in three lifetimes, yet they always wanted more. And they didn't care how they got it.

Older adults are also ideally suited for confidence crimes because they are often, unintentionally, a con artist's best friend. Take their money and in return they will usually remain silent.

Some refuse to report their misfortune for fear of playing into the stereotypical image of being incapable of handling their own affairs, thus providing their children with reason to consider moving them into a nursing home or other "retirement facility." Others have bought into the media hype suggesting that people who report their crimes will be tracked down by the criminals and murdered in their sleep. Not to be overlooked are those who simply don't care to make public the personal greed that led them down such a sinful path. As one man who had been conned out of several thousand dollars told the police, who were almost begging him to press charges, "Right now you and I know I made a jackass out of myself. If I press charges all my friends, neighbors, relatives, and business associates will know too."

The Get-Rich Quick Crowd

Combine greed, desire, impatience and foolishness, and you have created a group nicely suited for most gambling-related frauds, pyramid schemes, contest-winner scams, and various street hustles. Members of this group, having toiled long and hard, have suddenly discovered that there's seldom enough to make ends meet. Impatient, they now seek a path to instant wealth.

They shun involvement with any long-term investments or other financial ventures containing even the slightest hint of risk. Yet they think nothing of handing over hundreds of dollars to the numbers racket and its legal counterpart, state-sponsored lotteries. Never mind the

astronomical odds against them. The way they see it, their chances of becoming an instant millionaire are just as good as anyone else's.

No one is certain whether the desire for instant wealth came from human nature or was the creation of large companies trying to sell their goods by running endless contests and sweepstakes. Whatever its origin, the quest for instant wealth has created countless opportunities for con artists. No longer is it necessary to invest valuable time gaining the mark's confidence, because half the job is already completed by the marks themselves.

Imbued with a sense of urgency, they are all too eager to invest their money with anyone who says what they want to hear. And what they want to hear is that there is an easy way to make the money of their dreams. Only after they've exhausted their available income do they realize the differences between dreams and reality, common sense and foolish thinking. By then their only dream is that they might return to the good old days before they squandered their money.

Apprentice con artists trying to tap into this vast supply of eager spenders are faced with some hard work. With company- and state-sponsored contests, sweepstakes, giveaways, rub-offs, pull-offs, scratch-offs, peel-offs, old-fashioned punchboards, and just about every other gimmick imaginable, con artists have to be exceptionally creative to beat their competitors.

The Upper Crust

When you've got everything you want, there's always room for more. When you are wealthy, filthy rich becomes the next logical step. Couple this with the false belief that you're simply too educated, too dignified, or too intelligent to get taken in by some uncouth street con artist and you have the ideal sucker.

Con artists seeking large scores daily create sophisticated scams for sophisticated people. Their clients include doctors, lawyers, politicians, bankers, scientists, judges, investment brokers, retired magnates, and, occasionally, other con artists. Their scams of choice include large-scale investment opportunities, stock market schemes, fake-art scams, franchise frauds, and many others.

Those who target the upper crust long ago discovered that the higher one's social status, the easier he or she is to deceive. The reasons for this vary, but can most often be attributed to self-deception.

Such people allow themselves to believe that fraud is confined to those less worldly or less intelligent. They've read all about those silly pigeon-drop scams, bank-examiner schemes, and lottery frauds and can't imagine how anyone but a fool could fall for such nonsense. Some have even encountered perpetrators of these scams and are further convinced that no shoddily dressed, ill-mannered, street-hustling bastard could ever put one over on them. It just couldn't happen.

This observation is, of course, almost true. They are correct in assuming that they will never fall prey to such foolishness. What they obviously don't know is why. If they say it's because the scam itself is so obviously flawed, ask them to explain the mechanics of any one of those silly scams. What you're likely to receive is a demonstration on how to say nothing with words.

If ever they do uncover the truth about such scams, they will make two important discoveries. The first is that the scams are not as silly as they had imagined. Instead, they are carefully crafted, well-rehearsed, and expertly delivered performances. The second discovery will be that they missed the obvious: Those "silly scams" were never intended to work on them. They were tailored specifically for the intended marks, and them alone.

Their fervent belief that no crude, foul-smelling, ill-mannered hustler could ever con them renders the upper crust easy prey. Any con artist in possession of a decent suit and a modest stock of multisyllabic words can easily take these aristocrats for everything they have. As you might expect, there exists a great reluctance on the part of the upper crust to openly admit their lapses of good judgment. Those who do come forward insist they were deceived by one of the world's most proficient criminal masterminds, the kind that could have fooled even Sherlock Holmes.

The Business Sector

To show why con artists love the business sector, here's a brief story based on a case I investigated in March 1985. The case involved a tightly knit group of con artists from Texas who exploited major lending institutions.

Having but one purpose in mind—to obtain money—the group's leader, seasoned con artist Bobby Moresco, arrived in Milwaukee during the winter of 1985. Soon after his arrival, he became a frequent visitor at Jack Bannon's used car dealership in Madison, Wisconsin.

Using his years of experience, Moresco quickly located exactly what he was looking for: a greedy person eager to accept bribes. In this case it was Tom Ashton, the dealership's loan officer.

In three months from the middle of March to the middle of June, Moresco secured loans worth more than $120,000 on five cars. In each case Moresco used Ashton's contacts with a credit union, a savings and loan institution, and a national financing company to secure loans under fictitious names. He then paid off Ashton, distributed the cars to various accomplices in Texas and Wisconsin, and entered phase two of his well-planned scheme.

After obtaining multiple insurance policies on each of

the cars, again using fictitious names, there was a sudden rash of thefts and property damage claims. Because the various companies did not exchange much information among themselves, such double-dipping was indeed an easily obtained bonus.

Once Moresco had taken the insurance companies for all he could get, he focused his attention on the loan companies.

Having received no payments, the loan companies were desperate to speak to anyone who might help them out of their predicament. Moresco, of course, provided the out they so desperately sought.

Posing as a helpful citizen, Moresco and his accomplices began calling the loan companies. They purported that they knew where the cars were being stored and were willing—for a price—to assist in their recovery. Each company quickly agreed to pay a sizable "finder's fee." The companies clearly knew that they were simply paying a ransom to the con artist who duped them, but couldn't care less.

The entire scam might have worked had Moresco not made a foolish mistake. Bragging about one's exploits is common among con artists, however, doing so before the scam is completed is a foolish and often costly error. Proof of this observation came in the form of an anonymous call telling me about Moresco's ongoing caper. This story should end here, but there's more.

After arresting Moresco, obtaining a full confession, and finding all the stolen cars, I called the lending institutions. The purpose of these calls was a routine formality in which I would obtain the essential information needed to file a criminal complaint on their behalf. None would do so.

The reasoning offered for this refusal was that filing an official complaint would attract unwanted media attention. Such attention, they said, would only act as an inducement for other con artists. If true, I asked, how might these con artists view companies that, once taken, provided the cons with a cash bonus and then thanked them for the privilege of being conned by refusing to prosecute?

Because no answers were provided, we must again turn to the con artists for a few lessons in reality. As mentioned earlier, the perpetrators see no real difference between themselves and the rest of us, including so-called honest business professionals. As they see it, there are two basic reasons why companies daily ignore the money taken from them by professional con artists. They are:

First, as long as a company is making a profit, such losses are considered the price of doing business.

Second, the companies don't really lose anything. They simply pass their losses on to their customers in the form of higher prices. When the customers react, they simply transfer the blame for these increases onto con artists, shoplifters, and others.

The Rising Stars

Within every line of work you will find those halfway up the ladder of success who are eager to score points with the company's upper echelon. One of the best ways to do this is to display one's devotion to getting things done while saving the company money.

Such mid-level managers are proud of their abilities to survive amid the fierce competition reserved for the strong of heart. They are confident, observant, and willing to take calculated risks. But as any good con artist will tell you, they are also easy marks.

Like members of the upper crust, the rising stars are proud of their ability to spot a con game. And they do so with incredible consistency. However, their ability to do so only *after* rather than *before* they've been taken is a major flaw.

Evidence suggests the rising stars are also plagued with memory problems. Seldom, if ever, do any reports of a mid-level manager's encounter with a con artist reach the company executives. Instead, creative records manipulation, denial, and instant cover-ups quickly place the event into the "it-never-happened" category.

If only they would learn from their mistakes, perhaps they would stand a better chance of spotting the second team of swindlers who follow in the wake of their accomplices. Though hard to believe, taking such marks twice is a common event. Briefly, the come-back scam plays out in this fashion:

- First team takes the mark.
- Mark is allowed to wallow in complete panic.
- Second team of con artists arrive (as planned) and just happen to run into the mark at a local bar or restaurant.
- Second team gets mark to talk about his meeting with those awful con artists.
- Con artists present the mark with a solution to his problem.
- Mark takes offer, hands over more of the company's money, and is stung a second time.
- Mark can no longer hide the losses and loses his job.

Do the cons feel somehow responsible when a mark joins the ranks of the unemployed? Absolutely not. As a con artist once pointed out to me, "The only reason most suckers get fired is because they try conning their bosses. And let's face it, they're no good at it."

The True Believers

According to a Gallup Poll taken in 1991, half of the people in the United States believe in extrasensory perception (ESP), and one out of four believe that a psychic, an astrologer, a palm reader, a Tarot-card interpreter, or a phrenologist fingering the bumps on your head can foresee the future. One out of five Americans believe the medium can help you communicate with your deceased spouse, parent, child, mother-in-law, etc.

In 1990, I participated in a *Geraldo* show about fortunetellers. At one point Geraldo turned to the audience and asked how many of them believed that one person could effectively curse another. Fully 10 percent of the people sitting in the theater raised their hands. Admittedly, the audience was not a random sample such as those used by the Gallup organization, but the point is made. The American population contains a large percentage of people holding beliefs that make them vulnerable to con games. What's more important, many of these people are anxious to find someone who will prove that their beliefs are true and are willing to pay good money for the demonstration.

Knowing why so many people believe in these absurdities is not important. What you need to know is that tapping into these absurdities is easy, lucrative, and limited only by your imagination. Superstition, gullibility, blind faith, and a refusal to think are among this group's most usable peculiarities. Such traits are not limited to the uneducated, the lowly, and the poor. Even the wife of a past president of the United States was known to schedule her husband's daily activities based on the advice of her astrologer.

There are people who honestly believe they have extrasensory abilities, that they can foretell the future, that they can communicate with those who have passed over to the next world, and so on. They refuse to believe or even consider the extensive body of data documenting that all this is bunkum, which the dictionary defines as nonsense. We can distinguish between these true-believing bunkum artists and the bunco (con) artists who know damned well that they are running a scam and doing a good job of it, thank you.

Neither bunkum artists nor bunco artists would make a living at their art were it not for the many thousands of other true believers who willingly support them. These foolish people realize they themselves lack paranormal abilities but insistently maintain that others do. Successfully duping these people only requires that you say what they want to hear, show them what they want to see, and be ready to assist them during their efforts to ignore all evidence that threatens to destroy their beliefs.

If you somehow fail to satisfy their fantasies, simply transfer the blame onto them by saying they are not true believers. If they were, then everything would have gone as predicted. Although a useful tactic, it should serve to warn you that more work is needed on your listening skills. Find out what they want and then deliver.

If they choose to believe the future can be foretold, tell them their future. If they insist on believing that a person's worth can be determined by the position of the stars, then reach for the stars. If they believe in communicating with the dead, then learn to make tables rap and ectoplasm appear. Any good magic supply house will sell you the needed equipment.

Are these cruel and unfair portrayals? Perhaps. But try telling any of the true believers there is no Santa Claus and you will become their instant and eternal enemy. They do not want to hear anything that interferes with their takes on reality. If you don't provide for their needs, someone else will. If these adults insist on being fed a daily dose of nonsense, then it is your duty as a professional con artist to spare them from falling prey to self-deceived amateurs.

Always remember, the ability to play the part of a fool is in all of us. There are no exceptions. Whether caused by ignorance, superstition, greed, gullibility, or stupidity, foolishness is widespread and very much alive. So if you want to beat your competition, select your marks with great care and always be ready to offer them what they want. It's also wise to consider the words of James Howell, "Let us be thankful for the fools. But for them the rest of us could not succeed."

1. Laurence, Peter J. Dr., *Peter's Quotations: Ideas for Our Time.* New York: Morrow, 1977.

CHAPTER SIX

BIG CONS

"I never give them hell. I just tell the truth and they think it's hell."
—Harry S. Truman

To derive full benefit from this or any other chapter in this book, you must keep an open mind. Unfortunately, such open-mindedness is indeed rare. As an unknown author once noted, "In matters controversial, my perception's rather fine. I always see both points of view, the one that's wrong and mine."

To avoid such narrow-mindedness you must temporarily lay aside your personal beliefs and withhold any judgment until you have seen the con artist's world from his perspective. Do this and you will be in a much better position to decide if becoming a con artist is really what you want.

BIG CONS

Now let's have a look some of today's most popular big cons. Some of them will probably be familiar to you since they often make their way into the newspapers.

Pigeon Drop

Two closely related games are the bank-examiner scheme and the pigeon drop. As was mentioned earlier, these games rely heavily on the mark's congenital human frailty of wanting to get something for nothing. When properly presented these scams not only overcome the mark's good sense, but usually leave him begging to be swindled. Although today's version of the pigeon drop no longer resembles the original, its basic structure remains intact.

Usually working in pairs, the team finds their mark at a shopping center or other place where they are likely to find senior citizens. Seniors are not the only people who fall for this game, but they have proven to be the easiest to dupe.

Having found a suitable mark the team begins the game. The first con artist, (in this case a female and known as the *roper* or *catch*) approaches the mark and asks for directions, the time, or whatever it takes to catch and hold the mark's attention. After receiving an answer the roper will suddenly notice a package on a nearby bench. (The package is a prop planted shortly before the game began.)

"I wonder what this could be?" the roper asks. As the mark watches, the roper opens the package, looks inside, and gasps. Hugging the package tightly to her chest she turns to the mark and whispers, "There's money inside. Lots of money."

Now showing the mark what appears to be a stack of bills almost an inch thick, the roper discovers a note attached to one of the bills. Pulling out the note she hands it the mark instructing her to read it while she counts the money. This maneuver accomplishes two things. First, it distracts the mark's attention away from the money. This is necessary because the only money in the package is a Mich role. Second, it draws the mark further into the game.

The note read by the mark always gives the impression that the money is tainted and unlikely to be claimed by the crook who lost it. Here's a sample of a note taken from an arrested con artist:

> Harry, this is your share of the take from the dope deal. We already paid off the district attorney so you have to pay off the cops. See you in Las Vegas—Bill

When the mark informs the roper about the payoff note, the second con artist (a male known as the *cap*) appears and says to his accomplice, "Excuse me, I don't want to stick my nose in your business, but you really shouldn't be flashing all that money. People have been killed around here for a lot less."

The roper, maintaining her thespian ways, acts surprised, and then embarrassed. "We just found this money," she admits, "and we really don't know what we should do with it." She then gives the cap the note that she found with the money. After reading it, he voices his belief that the money is undoubtedly part of an illegal drug operation. How they should handle the money is beyond his area of expertise, but he knows someone who might help. "I work for an attorney who has an office only three blocks from here. If you'd like, I'll seek her advice on what you should do with the money."

While the cap is around the corner having a cup of coffee, the benevolent roper gives the mark some good news. "Hey, you were here when I found this money, so half of it is rightfully yours." Seldom does the mark turn down such a generous gift.

On his return the cap tells them that as far as his boss is concerned the money is theirs to keep. To this he adds one minor condition. "My boss did say that, to make it all legal, you must hold onto this money for at least a month. She doubts anyone will claim it, but the law says you have to wait."

This part of the game will continue for as long it takes to hook the mark. Once hooked, the discussion turns to dividing the money.

The roper suggests that since she's new in town and has yet to open a bank account, the mark should hold all the money until the end of the requisite waiting period. "Hold on!" exclaims the cap. "You two don't really know each other, so how can you be sure this guy won't be tempted to spend the whole bundle?"

Acting angered over such an accusatory remark the roper comes to the defense of the mark. "Look, mister, we really appreciate your help, and we'll even pay you for your time and trouble, but you have no right to pass judgment on this nice gentleman. I just know in my heart that he's honest."

"You're absolutely right," the cap says, "and I apologize for my remarks. Nevertheless, it would be a nice gesture on his part if he would show you a bit of good faith."

"What do you mean, good faith?" asks the roper.

"It's simple," he replies. "He just shows you that he has access to enough cash of his own and won't be tempted to spend any of your money."

Eager to end the minor problem that now separates him from his share of the loot the mark will usually offer proof of his financial stability without being asked. If no such proof is tendered the roper makes it known that she is giving serious thought to keeping all for the money for herself. Not wishing to dissolve the partnership the mark yields and agrees to be a "good faith" partner.

How much money the mark is about to lose depends on his storage facility. For the exceptionally greedy who hide their wealth from the evil tax collector, every dollar they have in their home will soon become the property of the con artists. Those who favor banks or other such financial institutions will be spared and only part with a sum no greater than $5,000. The size of this cash withdrawal has been field-tested and proven to attract the least amount of attention.

With the mark's money in hand the roper places it into a bag along with the Mich role. During a brief distraction the bag is switched for one containing blank paper. After exchanging telephone numbers and addresses the roper hands the bag over to the mark with instructions not to open it until he is safely home and out of harm's way. Such feigned concern is part of what the con artists call the kiss-off or blow-off. In other words, it's a delay tactic that affords them time to disappear. End of game.

Bank-Examiner Scheme

To the misinformed, bank-examiner schemes are nothing more than sleazy tactics used to rip-off poor, defenseless senior citizens. Who else but a scumbag would be so cruel as to gain the trust of such defenseless human beings and then take them for everything they've got? According to the con artists I've interviewed, this is an inaccurate and unjust portrayal of the scheme.

In the mark's version, the tale always includes these basic elements:

- The mark receives a telephone call from a man who says he's a bank examiner. The examiner reports his suspicions about a dishonest bank teller. Though embarrassing to the bank, it seems the teller is taking money from customers' accounts—including the mark's.
- The examiner then asks for his help in catching the teller in the act of stealing money.

- The mark is always satisfied with the examiner's story because he knows everything there is to know about the mark's personal bank account. And since the mark absolutely never discusses his personal finances with strangers, anyone with such details has to be legitimate.
- On the bank examiner's instructions the mark goes to the bank and withdraws $5,000 in cash. The entire transaction, according to the examiner, will be captured on the bank's security cameras.
- With cash in hand, the mark meets a police detective at home or at a prearranged meeting place. The officer examines the money, records the serial numbers, and apparently places the money into an envelope that is sealed and marked as evidence.
- Also per instructions, the victim returns to the bank the following day to deposit the money. Approaching the "dishonest" teller he asks that it be placed back into the appropriate account. The bank examiner says that this is the point where they will catch the teller in the act of stealing the money.
- The game is exposed with the opening of the envelope containing paper.
- The police are called to investigate. Soon after their interview with the mark, the cops conclude that this is definitely an inside job. Who else besides an insider would have so much information about the victim's bank account?
- The police waste countless hours investigating past and present employees, get nowhere, become frustrated, and place the case into the inactive files.

Con artists are quick to point out that their marks always omit two important pieces of information. For one, the mark *did* tell a stranger all about his personal banking habits. He did it about a week before the game began. This is when the con artist called him under the pretense of dialing the wrong number. The call went something like this:

Con Artist: "Hello, is this the Last Chance Bank?"

Mark: "No, you must have dialed the wrong number."

Con Artist: Oh, I'm terribly sorry, I'm just an old man who must be getting a bit careless. Are you an elderly person?"

Mark: "Yes, I'm certainly no youngster."

Con Artist: "Do you happen to know anything about banking?"

Mark: "Yes, but why do you ask?"

Con Artist: "Well my wife, God rest her soul, just passed away and left me wondering how it is that she managed what little money we have. She always took care of the banking, so I really don't have any idea how to read these darn bank statements."

Mark: "I know what you mean; they can be a bit confusing. How can I help you?"

Con Artist: "Well, what exactly are all those numbers on the checks all about?"

Mark: "Just a minute, let me get out my checkbook, and we'll go over it together."

This line of questioning continues until the con artist obtains details about the mark's account. Armed with this information he leaves town and returns several days later. He then calls posing as Mr. Bank Examiner and the game begins.

The other missing piece of information that almost all victims conveniently forget to mention is the reward money. Promising to credit his account with a $500 reward for his help in catching the dishonest teller is usually all that is required to hook the mark.

Should you find this game tempting you'll need a little more information before going into business. First, this is usually not a one-player game. The caller, or *setup*, is the brains of the operation and takes few risks. The *pickups*, your accomplices, will most often be apprentices who have yet to realize just how far out on the proverbial limb they are being placed. When these accomplices do become wiser, they soon set up games of their own. Don't forget what was said earlier about working with a partner. Never tell them more than they need to know. And you don't necessarily have to be completely honest with what information you do decide to give them.

Badge-Play Comeback

In the words of Jacob M. Braude, "There's no fool like an old fool—you can't beat experience." Although Braude was not referring to con games when he made this statement, he nevertheless nicely describes the marks who insist on repeating the same mistakes.

Also known as a *double-play* or *police follow-up*, the badge-play comeback is played exclusively with previous marks. Unlike many other police impersonator games, the badge-play requires full knowledge of the details used to take the mark during the initial game. Such details are an intangible commodity exchanged between con artists and are readily available on an even trade or cash basis.

Once in possession of the mark's profile the con artist can run the game solo or with the use of a partner. This is purely a matter of preference.

To gain an understanding of how and why the badge-play works, assume the role of the mark who was recently taken in a bank-examiner scheme.

It has been three weeks since you gave a stranger $5,000

of your hard-earned money. Your feelings of loss, anger, and utter disbelief occupy your every thought. You are an emotional wreck torn between unanswered questions and wishful thinking. "Just how stupid can I be?" you ask yourself.

Leaving your unanswered question behind, you focus your attention on a much greater need. Revenge. "I only wish the police would find those lousy crooks and hang them by their heels."

Then, appearing as a mysterious force with an ability to grant one's wishes, a messenger bearing good news arrives at your door.

The messenger says he's a detective from the police department. As proof of his identity he shows you an impressive gold badge. Just as you are about to ask him for more identification he presents you with some good news, "I'm glad to find you at home Mr. John, I wanted to be the first to tell you that we caught the team of con artists who took your money."

As you try to gather your thoughts he continues, "When we arrested them they still had all of your money, so we'll soon be returning it to you." Now relieved you listen—but you don't hear. If you did, you would take what the "detective" said next as the worst attempt at a scam every devised.

"There's only one problem," he says. "The money they took from you, the money you got from your bank, is counterfeit. But don't worry," he adds, "the bank has promised to make good on your losses."

From this point, the con artist asks you to accompany him to the police station to identify the suspects who took your money. He drives you to the station in what appears to be an unmarked squad car. The car is equipped with a spotlight and has a police scanner mounted under the dashboard (actually just a citizens band radio programmed to receive police broadcast frequencies).

On arriving at the police station the con artist leaves you seated in the car while he goes into to station to arrange the line-up. (Once inside he uses the rest room, asks the desk clerk a trivial question, or just walks in only to turn around and walk out.) He returns several minutes later and tells you that his captain said it would be OK to have you identify the suspects through photographs. That way you can avoid any unpleasant face-to-face confrontation with the suspects. To this he adds a sympathetic comment of understanding, "God knows, you've already suffered enough."

He then reaches into his suit pocket and produces a set of suspect photographs, none of which depict the guilty con artists. Unable to make identification, he tells you not to worry about it because the crooks already made a full confession and your identification isn't necessary. Your help, of course, is needed to catch the dishonest bank teller who gave you the counterfeit money.

The con artist now persuades you to escort him to your bank. Following his instructions you enter and withdraw $5,000 from your account. When you hand him the money he carefully examines several of the bills and declares them all to be counterfeit. You are issued a receipt and told to wait for further instructions. "By the way," the now smiling con artist says, "the bank has agreed to put a little extra into your account for being so helpful."

Three days later your feelings of loss, anger, and utter disbelief occupy . . . and you know the rest.

More Police Impersonators

If you ever wanted to become a cop, here's your golden opportunity. Why bother with tedious written examinations, strenuous physical tests, working your way through the ranks, or subjecting yourself to the many other unpleasant realities that cops have to live with to collect a paycheck, when there's a much easier way?

As a professional police impostor you will work whenever and wherever you want, free from laws, ordinances, rules, regulations, or policies. What's more, your income will exceed that of the highest-paid cop in the nation.

Unlike the badge-play comeback, your mark need not have been a previous player. In fact, first-time marks are preferred. Then, too, most of the senior citizens you will target have never had any contact with the police and have no idea what to expect. The only role-playing on your part consists of wearing a halfway decent suit (no white socks—please!), and speaking in a calm and authoritative manner. To this add an impressive badge and they'll believe anything you say. (Incidentally, official-looking badges are a dime a dozen. You can obtain them through catalogs or surplus stores. Even dime stores carry badges that often look better than the ones issued to the real cops.)

After you have acquired the proper credentials you will locate a market or other place of business frequented by senior citizens. Position yourself so you can view all who exit the store. The ideal mark should be alone and look like a professional victim. Professional victims are easy to spot because they walk with their heads down, shoulders slumped, and have no conception of their immediate surroundings.

On finding such a person, approach and quietly identify yourself as a police detective. If the mark accepts your assumed role, immediately explain that you are investigating the activities of a local crime syndicate. The syndicate is spreading large amounts of counterfeit currency throughout the neighborhood, and it is suspected that these crooks are working in partnership with the area merchants.

You now ask the mark for permission to examine the currency he has received as change from purchases made at any of the local stores. When the money is handed to you examine it, then shake your head and say, "Just what I was afraid of, this money is counterfeit."

Now, with an expression of great concern, break the bad news. "Gee, I don't know how to explain this to you, but once you accept bogus money from anyone you're stuck with it. The banks will take it from you because it's the law, but they won't give you anything in return, and neither will the government." Then add, "I might be able to help you out. If I tell my captain that you are helping me with the investigation I can probably get our department to exchange all of your bad money for good money."

With no clear choices open to them most marks will gladly become your temporary partner. Since you are such a thorough detective you will, of course, offer to examine any other money that he has at home. You will only offer these added services after finding out that he lives alone.

On your arrival at the mark's home you will conduct an official examination of his currency and certify all of it as worthless paper. From here, you will give the mark an official receipt and your promise to return in a few days with the replacement money.

If you didn't immediately notice the risk involved in this game, then by no means should you try to run any games on your own. Finish reading this book, read it again, and then proceed with great caution.

Risk always increases in direct proportion to the amount of exposure. In the present scenario you were with the mark from the point of contact until the kiss-off. This increased your chances of being spotted by the mark's neighbors or anyone else who might stop by for a visit. Worse yet, if one of those nosy neighbors became suspicious and called the cops you would—just like the con artist who ran this game—be caught in the act.

If you feel cheated because I said this was an easy game to run, please pay closer attention. Never have I said, nor will

I ever say, that any game is without risk. As already noted, risk is what makes confidence games worthwhile. To misquote a familiar aphorism, "Getting there is half the fun."

Mail-Order Scams

As children we have all sent away for those treasures advertised on the backs of cereal boxes. What we usually received in return for our blissful anticipation and a goodly portion of our modest allowance was a piece of plastic junk. Since then, we have demonstrated our inability to learn from history and continue to place orders for X-ray eyeglasses, pet rocks, Veg-O-Matics that slice, dice, and pulverize our food, and other such wonders of the world.

That we are somehow being conned by slick advertisers never occurs to us. Instead we blame ourselves for being so childish. And the con artists who thrive on such assumed culpability are still with us today and promise to remain with us for many generations to come.

In keeping with this long-standing tradition I now offer you a chance to make your dreams come true. Read the advertisement on the next page and assume that you simply could not live without the product and have just placed an order.

Six weeks later the XRT-7 arrives at your home. In this scenario you live on the last page of this book, so turn to that page and enjoy your newly acquired treasure.

Investment Schemes

Setting the tone for a *Forbes* magazine article in the spring of 1985 entitled "The Smarter They Are, The Harder They Fall," the author wrote, "The American public is better educated and better informed than ever. But here's a paradox: The more people know, the dumber and more careless they seem to get about their investments."

No smarter today than they were in 1985, the American

public continues to hand over hundreds of millions of dollars to investment-scheme con artists every year. This occurs despite the continual flow of articles, books, and

television and newspaper reports exposing these schemes. Why? Because every scheme exposed appears to be different from the last.

Marks who fall prey to, or have heard about, land-investment schemes usually become easy prey for stock schemes. Others who get fleeced in a pyramid scam think nothing of trying their luck at gold and silver investments. And the list goes on.

The common denominator for each of the hundreds of schemes now used is seldom noticed by anyone except the con artists. In plain English, most people do not understand what is being offered to them and only hear what they want to hear. If any of this sounds familiar, you've been paying attention.

As we have already learned, when someone wants to believe a particular thing is possible, then believe it they will. Regardless of how irrational their beliefs might be, and despite any amount of evidence to the contrary, they refuse to abandon what for them is comfortable to believe.

Learning that con artists use such beliefs to create successful investment schemes is not an amazing discovery. What should be considered amazing are the marks who refuse to learn from their past mistakes. Perhaps this insistence stems from their inability to understand exactly how and why these schemes work. As professional con artists you cannot afford such ignorance.

Here's a quick test of your ability to devise an investment scheme of your own. Read this familiar adage and make a note of what you think it means.

If it sounds too good to be true, then it probably is.

If your mind went blank, you were not thinking through the mind of a professional con artist. If you had been, you would have taken this adage to mean that if the mark thinks it's too good to be true, you failed to devise a plausible tale.

Although you are allowed great latitude and artistic

freedom when creating your schemes, they must contain some element of plausibility. Since we have already talked about state-operated lotteries, let's look at the psychology that makes it all work.

There are two indisputable facts associated with the odds of winning the lottery jackpot. The first is that the odds of winning are anything but favorable. The second is that someone will win. Playing down the unfavorable and emphasizing the improbable is what con artists do best.

As you can see, one way to create a believable scheme involves basing it on something that could or has already occurred regardless of how improbable a repeat occurrence might be. Another way is to overstate something that could or might happen to those wise enough to lend you their trust. To demonstrate this technique, here's some selected text taken from an advertisement recently sent through the mail to thousands of potential marks. I've added my comments in parentheses.

> Dear Friend,
> I'd like you to be my guest at a very exciting event coming soon to your area. Mark your calendar for ____. Choose your most convenient day and time and join us at the ____.
> I'm not exaggerating when I say that this event could (the key word here is *could*) change your life forever. Yet it takes just a little of your time, there's absolutely no obligation, and it costs you nothing. (Outright lies.)
> You'll find out about an amazing money-making opportunity that can give you the personal freedom you want. A business that takes you just a few hours a week and starts filling your pockets with cash in as little as 60 days. (The word cash could mean anything—$1 bills, nickels, etc.) You'll see how easy it

is to start money flowing into your bank account every day of the week.

If you're a bit skeptical, I can't blame you. It sounds too good to be real. But you'll see proof that every word I'm saying is true. (This technique is used to gloss over the obvious fact that there's a scam in progress. If you can't hide it, then highlight it. The promised proof of validity will never be delivered.)

You'll meet and talk with people who are already living the good life thanks to this same business opportunity. (You'll meet the con artist's accomplices.) They're people just like you, who longed for wealth and independence—the only difference is, they're making their dreams come true! (How do they know you're not already wealthy? Answer: They bought a mailing list containing the names of middle-income people.) Their lives changed forever when they accepted their special invitation—just like the one you're holding.

Sincerely yours,
M.D. Henningson
Call today,
Automated Systems, Inc. 1-800-555-0000

This come-on continues for several pages, and is another tactic used to talk a lot without saying anything. To personalize this general mailing the con artist simply used this bit of rhetoric: "This invitation has only been sent to a select group of people who have expressed a serious interest in making money." Few ever wonder how a stranger could know about their personal "serious interests." No less astounding are the number of marks who attend such meetings, especially since there is no direct mention of what type of amazing business could produce such financial bliss. The only clue in the ad you just read consisted of two words, "automated systems."

Automated systems could mean any number of things, but in this case it meant vending machines. Con artists are able to run schemes that center around this business because there are many honest vending-machine distributors who have indeed helped their clients net tidy profits: Not easy, overnight, guaranteed profits, but profits nonetheless.

Con artists mimic the honest company's tactics for locating investors. However, since they don't have to deliver what they promise they can afford to offer their clients much more. What a mark receives for his investment in the con artist's vending machine dealership is an opportunity to attend a truly amazing performance.

If you can envision a gathering that is teeming with the enthusiasm of a full-blown religious revival designed to reawaken religious faith, then you will have some sense of the spirit of the game. To this enthusiasm add a group of professional con artists who would be the envy of every carnival pitchman whoever lived, and you will understand why there is no chance for survival for those foolish enough to enter the con man's lair.

Once you're on their turf, they will make more promises than politicians running for office. In a similar fashion they will even make good on a few of their promises. In the present scheme, they could provide the marks with vending machines of their own. What's more, they might even consider providing places to install them.

The marks will, of course, pay dearly for these less-than-new machines and will eventually discover that their equipment shares a space with many others just like them. This works on the same principle used by some major corporations. They will sell you a business franchise but fail to mention the 10 other dealerships that will be your close neighbors.

Another twist to this scheme would be to get the sucker's money up front and then disappear. In either case, your earnings will depend on the plausibility of your performance.

Fortune-Telling

If you are seriously thinking about becoming a professional con artist but don't like to travel, this scam is just for you. In all fairness I will warn you that this particular form of deception is difficult to master. If, for any reason, you doubt your ability to maintain a deception for extended periods of time, then skip this game and select one that matches your abilities. If, however, you are confident, adventurous, and have a keen eye for details, read on.

Fortune-telling is not merely a fraud—it's an art form. Because you will establish yourself as a "legitimate servant of the people" and operate from a semi-permanent base of operation, you cannot afford to make foolish mistakes.

For advice on conducting a near perfect fortune-telling scheme we will turn to the experts—the Gypsies. With more than two decades of close contact with these polished professionals, I can say with the utmost confidence that their ability to separate marks from their money is quick, efficient, and predictably consistent. Although they work in plain view and take in unbelievable amounts of cash, they have perfected an ability to deflect any serious attention from their activities. Duplicating such proficiency takes time, practice, and the following information:

- Always view fortune-telling for what it is: a means of separating fools from their money. Believe that such powers exist and you are a bigger fool than your marks.
- Adjust your approach to fit the marks. If they are simply curious, entertain them with the types of

universally applicable advice found in the daily astrology columns. "Today is a good day to renew old relationships" and other such nonsense will suffice. For this service charge a modest fee, keeping in mind that these fools are crucial to your ultimate success. They serve to strengthen the myth that fortune-telling is little more than harmless entertainment. More importantly, they will also become your best advertisers and steer bigger marks your way.

- Save your best material for your biggest marks. Your biggest marks are those with lots of money and a belief that their present problem is beyond their control. Those problems can include physical illnesses, grief, depression, job-related difficulties, feelings of inadequacy, a faltering love relationship, and much more.

- Learn to read your marks. Once you have unlocked the secrets of reading a mark you will possess an ability to fool anyone, anywhere, anytime—guaranteed! But this is where the going gets tough. What you are being asked to master is the ability to conduct what is commonly known as a cold reading: the careful observation of how others respond to what you say, and then letting those responses guide your subsequent remarks. All of your marks, like you, constantly give off tremendous amounts of information. They do this through their body language, accent, clothing, jewelry, mood, posture, and so on. Using these clues in conjunction with what the mark has already told you during your pleasant—and very important—initial contact, you will reveal information about his or her past that no one should know who hasn't been there. The mark will not recall telling you anything and will therefore be amazed by your powers.

- Regardless of what problems plague your mark you will always credit them to some curse placed on him by an evil-spirited person. As proof of this curse do the unexpected and perform a magic trick. That's right, a magic trick. Not a mild-mannered trick where rabbits are pulled from a hat, or where you ask them to pick a card, but a trick that will scare them out of their wits. Turning water to blood is a favorite, and can be purchased from any magic shop. Another favorite involves the use of an egg. The egg, as you will tell the mark, is the source of life. It can help restore happiness and remove the evil from within. In using the egg trick, place the egg against the mark's chest. Then say, "Here is an egg that has been lying close to your heart, making you healthier, taking away the evil from within you. See!" Now smash the egg on a table in front of the mark's eyes. When he flinches, remove the bits of wet hair or any other evil looking substance you have palmed in your hand, and work it up from the bottom of the egg. With some practice this maneuver will make it appear that the evil mass is being pulled from within, rather than being pushed up through, the egg. When the mark gasps, inject a well-rehearsed chant or prayer.
- Having demonstrated your multifarious powers it is now time to rid the mark of both his curse and his money. As you will carefully point out, the curse removal business is complicated and very costly.

A complete list of the methods used to extract a mark's money at this point would be interminable. Having brought your mark this far proves that you have more than enough skill to take his money. So much skill, in fact, that you must avoid the temptation to take him for all he has.

Deprive a mark of his entire life savings and your next customer will be wearing a uniform: a police uniform. To help you resist this temptation keep in mind that the average fortune-teller who practices restraint easily brings in over $500,000 a year. And that's during a bad year.

When you need additional encouragement to avoid temptation, think about your investment. Setting up and maintaining a semi-permanent base of operation costs time and money. Intentionally jeopardizing such an operation is both foolish and unnecessary.

In many communities throughout the country fortune-telling is a con game that is openly embraced and encouraged. Even when regulations, laws, or ordinances governing such activities exist, they are either ineffective or completely ignored. Any serious law enforcement intervention will only occur when sufficient numbers of marks complain. And this is a problem easily avoided if you exercise restraint and common sense.

Business Schemes

You will have noticed by now that con artists view nothing in an ordinary way. Their view of the business world is no exception. One of the more humorous descriptions came from a seasoned con artist who told me that major corporations are like cows waiting to be milked. By way of explanation he provided a few facts about cows: they are in abundance, they don't complain when being milked (unless they are not dairy cows), they provide useful products, and they are used and abused by almost everyone. Likewise, there is no shortage of companies, businesses, and corporations that provide a useful product (money), won't complain when being fleeced, and are abused daily by employees, lawyers, stockholders, customers, suppliers, lenders, accountants, partners, tax-collectors, and competitors.

Other con artists see a business institution as a priceless collection of individual suckers under one roof. The only relevance of a company's size is that the bigger the company the better the con artist's chances of finding someone who doesn't know what they're doing. Except for the stiff competition, business schemes are the easiest, safest, and most profitable.

To overcome your competitors (other con artists, company employees, lawyers, stockholders, and so on) you must be first and you must be different. Being the first to use a new or repackaged scheme will usually catch most business people off guard. Try to run a game they've already discovered and you face the risk of getting caught. Even though proficient con artists can find a way around a company's fraud prevention programs, these measures do make the game more difficult. So be first and avoid the hassles.

Being different also has its advantages. When attempting to use a game that has an ancient history you must make every effort to modify the illusion. These alternations need not be mind-boggling, just different.

By way of illustration, yesteryear's bogus billings are today's phony invoices. Although the scheme is anything but a secret, it is estimated that businesses dole out more than $100 million annually to con artists they never meet.[1]

The scam often begins with a phone call. Under the pretense of conducting a company-authorized investigation on ways to save money, the con artist asks to speak with an office manager or other middle-management employee. From that employee the con artist obtains details on the company's business practices.

The questions asked always include one intended to extract the information the con artist needs to run the scam. In this example the con artist obtains information about the company's yellow-page listing, how much the service costs, and the date the company is usually billed.

U.S BUSINESS SERVICES
YELLOW PAGES

CLASSIFIED TELEPHONE DIRECTORY

Nationwide Directory Publishers

YOUR LISTING INFORMATION SHOWN BELOW

**ABC SYSTEMS, INC
332 MINOR STREET
TAMPA, FLORIDA 54332**

TELEPHONE   (305) 999-1234

Account Number	**94566887**
Payable by due date:	**$ 99.45**
Due Date:	**June 16, 2000**
Payable after due date:	**$117.00**

AVOID CANCELLATION OF YOUR LISTING BY PROMPTLY RETURNING LOWER PORTION
WITH PAYMENT. THANK YOU.

LISTING INFORMATION AS SHOWN BELOW

**RETURN THIS PORTION WITH YOUR
PAYMENT**

**ABC SYSTEMS, INC
332 MINOR STREET
TAMPA, FLORIDA 54332**

TELEPHONE (305) 999-1234

FAX NUMBER (__)_____
FREE LISTING ( )_____

**MAKE CHECK PAYABLE TO:
U.S. TELEPHONE COMPANY
PO BOX 123 * MADISON, WI 53244**

Account Number	94566887
Payable by due date:	**$ 99.45**
Due Date:	**June 16, 2000**
Payable after due date:	**$117.00**
FOR OFFICE USE ONLY	

DIRECTORY   ADVERTISING   GETS   RESULTS!

This is not a bill. This is a solicitation. You are under no obligation to pay unless you accept the offer and allow us to publish your telephone numbers in our directory.

Let's assume that the company's yellow-page service is U.S. Telephone Company. The listing costs the company $99.45 a month, which is payable on the 16th. Using this information the company receives the invoice shown on the following page.

If you pay attention (which is something the companies who pay for these phony invoices fail to do) you notice that this is not an invoice. Made to look like an invoice, this solicitation intentionally fails to mention anything about the circulation figures or where the directories are distributed. This omission is only important if you decide to play the game for as long as possible.

Choosing the semi-legal approach you must print and distribute copies of the directory to the companies that paid you. When these companies discover that they are only advertising to other advertisers they will complain, but have no legal recourse. After all, you never said (nor did anyone ask) how many directories would be printed or where they would be sent.

Though unpleasant, it will also be necessary to follow (or work around) a few silly regulations promulgated by the U.S. Postal Service. In brief, those regulations state that any mailed bill, invoice, or statement of account due that is really a solicitation must display a disclaimer in 30-point type or larger. How can you defeat these regulations? If yours is a hit-and-run operation, ignore them. If you've created a semi-legal operation, ignore them, but in a creative way. Here's how:

Be human and make a mistake. Tell the printer to use 9-point print on the disclaimer. You will, of course, fail to notice this "mistake" until it is brought to your attention. When this occurs you will either apologize and promise to correct the unfortunate error, or leave town. Better yet, don't allow yourself to get caught.

Use a mail drop when setting up your business. Having rented such a facility, locate someone who, for a modest fee, is willing to pick up your mail and meet with you at any of several prearranged meeting spots.

Given the corporate philosophy mentioned earlier of not prosecuting because it might encourage others to duplicate the scam, getting caught in the act does not mean the end of your career. Just threaten to go public with the details of your scam unless the company drops charges. Tell them you'll write a bestseller and have it promoted on Oprah Winfrey's show. Do whatever it takes to intimidate them.

Hispanic Lotto Scam

Sharing a common heritage (which means that you must speak Spanish and look Hispanic) is what makes the *Hispanic Lotto Scam* a major success. Recalling how life was before their arrival to America, the marks are vulnerable to anyone in possession of a plausible tale. And this is where you and your accomplice begin the game.

Appearing lost and confused you approach your mark and ask for assistance in locating an attorney. The slip of paper you hand him bears the name of a nonexistent law firm. While the mark examines the paper your accomplice (the cap) approaches and offers assistance. On being given the name of the law firm the cap immediately says that the firm has a bad reputation for cheating Hispanics. The cap then asks you why you want to do business with such dishonorable people.

You now disclose that you hold a winning lottery ticket but fear any attempt to collect the winnings will reveal your illegal alien status and lead to your deportation. The cap then offers to cash the ticket on your behalf. You then simultaneously accept and reject the offer. Openly realizing that you don't know these people you counter with a better suggestion.

Although the ticket is worth $20,000 you are a person of modest means and would be willing to sell them the ticket for only $5,000. The cap immediately offers to give you the money but you intercede on behalf of the mark. "Look," you say, "this person was nice enough to help me out, and I would feel much better if you both shared the ticket. That way all of us will benefit from my good fortune."

The cap, who is agreeable to everything, has no problem with giving you $2,500. And neither will the mark. With the mark's contribution in-hand, the cap suddenly becomes a trusting soul and allows the mark to cash the ticket while he waits at a nearby restaurant. While the mark is inside the store learning that the lottery ticket is worthless, you and the cap should already be miles away.

This game can be played for much higher stakes and is dependent on the degree of the mark's gullibility and the size of his or her bank account. Upping the ante also requires the use of a more refined prop. In this case, the lottery ticket must be altered to reflect the winning numbers. This forgery need only be good enough to pass a casual inspection by the mark. Anyone who insists on a close inspection is given the standard line: "If you don't trust me, then to hell with you! I'll keep all the money for myself."

1. Whitlock, Charles R. *Easy Money*. New York: Kensington Books, 1994.

CHAPTER SEVEN

SHORT CONS

*"Tain't what a man don't know that hurts him;
it's what he knows that just ain't so."*
—Frank McKinney Hubbard

Just how long does it take to commit a short con? Look at your watch and note the time. Now see how long it takes you to read the following paragraph:

Someone rings your doorbell. You walk to the door and observe a uniformed United Parcel Service delivery person. On opening the door she hands you a $49.95 C.O.D. package. Assuming someone else in your household placed an order but forgot to mention it, you hand over the required cash and watch the delivery truck disappear down the road. On opening the package you discover it contains an inexpensive book, novelty item, or other low-grade merchandise. You've just fallen prey to a C.O.D. scam. Elapsed time: 35 seconds.

Another version of this scheme takes advantage of a death in the family. Reading obituaries with mercenary interest the con artist notes the hobbies and affiliations of the deceased. A trip is then made to a second-hand book-store where appropriate cheap volumes of a Bible, a concordance, or a commentary for the active church member, a history of masonry for the Freemason, a book of patterns for a member of the quilting bees, and so on, are purchased and sent C.O.D. to the address of the deceased. Each shipment is priced far beyond that of the contents. Usually the bereaved pays the C.O.D. charges, assuming that someone who cannot now protest ordered the book.

SHORT CONS

As the name implies, short cons are quick, in-and-out hustles designed to get you and the mark's money away from the scene as quickly as possible. In the first example, your mark will never even see your face.

Bail-Bond Scheme

Having done your homework and knowing something about your mark's family you phone their home and identify yourself as a police officer. You claim to have arrested one of their relatives who requested that you call and ask if they could wire some bail money. Although you are too busy to answer their questions, you do have time to instruct them on how to wire the money by way of Western Union. Those instructions are that they send the money under a code number so that one of your officers can pick it up and post the requisite bond.

What if the mark becomes suspicious and calls the police? The worst that could happen is that the intended victim will not send you the money. With more than 18,000 Western Union agents throughout the country and no way of knowing which one you will use to collect the money, any effective police intervention is unlikely. How unlikely? During my 30 years of investigating confidence crimes I have yet to arrest anyone for their involvement in this particular game.

The short cons we will now examine contain a greater degree of risk. You will now come face-to-face with your mark.

The Block Hustle

Should reading about this next game cause you to feel the slightest bit of sympathy for the so-called victims, then shame on you. The proper response would be to revere the block hustle as a public service worthy of our encouragement and complete support.

To state the obvious, there exists in this country a very sizable market for stolen goods. The market consists of thieves and the buyers of stolen goods. While we publicly pretend not to know why a thief would steal 50 video recorders, 60 televisions, or hundreds of cases of disposable diapers, we privately realize that they do so only to meet the demands of the "honest citizens" who buy and create the market for those items. If this were not the case then the *block hustle* could not possibly be as successful as it is.

To run a block hustle you will have to make a minor investment and procure the services of someone in possession of a plastic-wrap machine and a large quantity of empty merchandise boxes. After obtaining the necessary props you will fill all but one of the boxes with just enough rocks or old books to approximate the weight of the sale item. The remaining box will be left open and contain an actual sample of the item intended for sale.

Having loaded the packaged items into your truck or van you will now drive to a busy parking lot and begin approaching your marks. During the presentation of your tale you must offer the marks a deal they can't refuse. In other words, a price far below the market value. The plausibility of your tale is created when you inform the marks (either directly or indirectly) that what they are buying is stolen merchandise.

When confronted by interested buyers who insist on examining the goods, show them the display item and say that opening the other cartons would lower their selling price. Should the mark pay for the item and attempt to examine the contents, pretend to observe an approaching police officer and flee the scene.

Perhaps you can now understand why every honest citizen should feel indebted to the con artists who practice this game. Unlike those unsophisticated thieves who steal and give nothing in return, con artists take nothing and help to reduce the demand for such property by teaching their marks a lesson they won't soon forget.

Precious Pet Scam

Are you a lover of animals? If so, you probably have a way with them and can easily steal one for use as a prop in the *precious pet scam*.

Having located a cat or dog, preferably a pedigree, borrow it from its owner and visit a local bar. While inside the bar spend a few dollars on drinks and gain the bartender's respect through generous tips. Just before leaving ask the bartender if he or she would be willing to watch your pet for 20 minutes while you attend an important business meeting.

Several minutes after leaving the pet in the bartender's care your talkative accomplice enters the bar and eventually mentions his fondness for pets—more specifically a pet just like the one you left behind. The bartender will most likely highlight the coincidence of his encounter with the previous customer and allow you to see the pet. On seeing this adorable creature your accomplice immediately offers to buy it for a sizable amount of money. The bartender will say that the pet is not his to sell.

Not willing to accept rejection your accomplice provides the bartender with his name, telephone number, and instructions to call him if the owner is interested in selling the pet.

When you reenter the bar some time later be sure to openly complain about the business deal that just went sour and left you hopelessly in debt. Recognizing the perfect opportunity to net a quick profit, the bartender will offer to buy your pet. "Look, you need the money, and I absolutely love this dog, so why don't you allow me to help you out here?" He will, of course, offer you much less than the amount cited by your accomplice. After some dickering you acquiesce and accept whatever the bartender is willing to pay.

You and your accomplice won't stick around to determine the pet's ultimate fate, but it could include a quick release, a sale to an unsuspecting customer, or a debut as the bar's newest sandwich item.

Though hard to believe, this particular scam was so successful for its inventor, Yellow Kid Weil, that he easily fleeced an estimated 10 suckers a day. He claimed this scam alone provided him and his accomplices with more than $7 million during a 40-year period.

Truckload Scam

Throughout this book I have cautioned you about placing too much trust in an accomplice. To this I will add some information seldom available to anyone but a seasoned con artist.

When in need of partners, consider using your marks by having them do most of the work. Here's an example of how this can be accomplished:

Place a telephone call to a shipping or receiving department of any large company of your choice. On reaching an employee, claim that you have conducted a lot of business with the company. Be sure to mention that because the company's employees have always treated you fairly, you now want to offer then a special deal as a way of saying thanks.

Your company, so your tale goes, is preparing for an inventory audit and must move a large volume of televisions, video recorders, and microwave ovens. You have been authorized to sell all of these items at company cost. The only hitch is that the minimum sale on each item is in lots of 50.

After encouraging the mark to locate interested employees you provide a list of the brand names on the merchandise along with the exact giveaway prices on each item. Promising to call the mark back in one week, you hang up the phone and relax.

After the mark has prepared the order you instruct him to rent a truck and meet you at the loading dock of a reputable company. When the mark arrives you collect his money and tell him to back the truck into an empty loading bay while you go inside to open the door. The only door you will be opening is the one leading out of the building to the area where you parked your car in preparation for an immediate getaway.

Pot Game

Just for fun, here's a quick way to pick up some pocket change while providing the sucker and all who watch with a bit of entertainment.

During a conversation with a bar patron, ask him if he has ever played the pot game. Once you've captured his interest explain the rules of the game. RULE ONE: Both players place a $5 bill on the bar. RULE TWO: Both players will be allowed to bid on the pot with the pot going to the highest bidder. Your RULE: (not mentioned): You will always start the bidding at $5. The next bet, the sucker's bet, ends the game. Take the fool's money, and while acting disappointed declare him the winner.

For the sake of clarity, let's say that after your bid of $5 the sucker bids $8. Immediately tell the sucker the pot is his and collect the $8. That represents the $5 you put in plus a $3 profit. Most suckers will fail to realize their loss. As they see it, they just gave you $8 and have retrieved $10 from the bar. For them, this appears to be a $2 profit. The principle behind this game is the exact opposite of what occurs during a change-raising routine. Instead of you counting the store's money as if it were yours, the sucker in the pot game mistakenly counts your $5 as if it were his. The only notable difference is their "error" is unintentional.

Oak Tree Game

Rooted in deception, this particular scam is in a class all its own. On approaching homeowners you will offer to sell them oak trees at a price far below that of the local garden stores. You will even go one step further and plant any trees the mark buys at no extra cost.

On the day of the planting you arrive with your truck, some shovels, and the bargain oak trees. After carefully planting the trees you collect your money and move on to the next mark. Several days later the newly planted trees die—each and every one of them. And what do you think the mark will discover when examining the damaged goods?

No, the trees weren't diseased or in any way damaged. The problem is that the trees were really well-trimmed branches placed into soil and wrapped in burlap to disguise their lack of a root system.

Pickpocket Schemes

To be up front, I have no intention of telling you how to pick pockets. I mention the topic, here, only because of the tendency that many people have to view these thefts as confidence crimes. They are not.

When properly executed, pocket picking is indeed an art that requires speed and a deftness of touch. These skills, however, do nothing to transform a common act of theft into a spectacular con game. As D.W. Maurer, a noted authority on frauds, once noted, "[C]onfidence men [and women] are the aristocrats of the grift [confidence games] by reason of their superior intelligence, their striking personal attributes, not the least of which is a superb knowledge of human psychology, and their very large incomes." Although written in 1940, Maurer's observation continues to serve as an accurate distinction between crude thefts and the sophisticated psychological gamesmanship practiced by professional con artists.

CHAPTER EIGHT

ALLIES, ENEMIES, AND SURVIVAL TACTICS

"A man can't be too careful in his choice of enemies."
—Oscar Wilde

Strip con artists of their chimerical image as aristocrats of the criminal world and they are revealed as contemptible, self-serving thieves. They lie, cheat, and make a mockery of the trust that is so necessary to the survival of our society. Before you scream foul, know that con artists and their victims accept this view as a basic fact of life. Certainly not a fact that any good con artist will openly agree with, but a fact nevertheless.

If you believe, even for a moment, that cheating another person out of his property is anything less than a dishonest act, then you are the victim of what George Orwell, the late author of *1984*, aptly described as "doublethink." Orwell explained this as the ability to maintain two contradictory beliefs in the mind at the same time without conflict. Doublethink is not saying the opposite of what you believe, says Orwell, but thinking the opposite of what is true.

Allow yourself to mis-think in this fashion and you are just another sucker. Stealing from others is theft. It is not an honorable activity, nor is it an alternative to holding an honest job. If this reality troubles you, you have a conscience that will probably render you unfit to enter the world of a professional, and quite unconscionable, con artist.

IN THOSE WE TRUST

Why would self-sufficient, intelligent people allow you—a conniving thief—to do all their thinking? At this point you should already know the secret behind all successful schemes. Although it has been mentioned several times before, this crucial point warrants additional coverage:

Most people only hear and see what they agree with. All other information is rejected and ignored.

Let's suppose for a moment that you are afflicted with a life-threatening disease. Having subjected yourself to months of painful and unsuccessful treatments someone suddenly appears and claims to have found a foolproof cure. Because you want desperately to believe that your suffering is about to end, you will hear everything they have to say on the subject but your mind will be elsewhere. Instead of listening to the details you will be busy making plans for your pain-free future. When all is said and done your mind will manufacture information that never existed. Because this self-made information complements your wishful thinking you will not realize your error until it's too late.

To illustrate the difference between hearing and listening, here's a rather difficult intelligence test you can use to prove the validity of this observation. Although you will be looking at, rather than hearing, the words printed on this page the process is identical because it requires you to think. The materials needed for this test are a penny, a dime, and a nickel. Place these items on a table and look at them as you answer the following test question:

> Jack's parents have three children. If one is named Penny (focus your attention on the penny), and another is named Nicole (look at the nickel), what is the name of the third child? (Look at the dime).

If you supplied the correct name (to be revealed shortly) on the first attempt, then you are indeed a very attentive individual. If, however, you are a member of the majority, then you probably came up with Dimetrious, Dimwit, and many other incorrect answers. Here's why.

Rather than providing you with something you wanted to hear I did just the opposite and used words that always seem to evoke fear. Those words were *test* and *difficult*. I chose them for diversionary purposes. The use of the small change was just another tactic for getting you to think about something other than what I said—a goal of all con artists.

If you were unable to answer the test question, take a few moments to examine your feelings. If you tried to provide the correct answer, you probably felt frustrated. On telling you that the correct answer is "Jack" you might now find it impossible to believe that you could have so easily missed the obvious. After all, I did say "Jack's parents . . ."

While all of this is still fresh in your mind, consider how a fraud victim feels when discovering that he not only failed to grasp the obvious, but also paid dearly for the experience. As you might imagine, he won't be too eager to share his gullibility with others. To the contrary, most victims are likely to keep their encounters with con artists forever a secret. In those instances where they do come forward with their tale of woe, seldom will it resemble the actual occurrence. More likely are fanciful stories intended to lessen the degree of their gullibility. Call it saving face, salvaging one's dignity, or whatever else you choose, this denial process ultimately protects you from the likelihood of being held accountable for your actions.

To maintain this support, albeit unintentional, from your victims requires a firm grip on the realities of your chosen profession. Treat any notion that you are something less than a well-dressed thief as a warning. Ignore such warnings and you are just another loser.

The Image Makers

When you obtain money by misleading people you are called a con artist, a thief, or a cheat. When you do this on a broad scale it's called journalism. So prevalent is this practice that it appears in the dictionary:

> *yellow journalism* (noun) Journalism that exploits, distorts, or exaggerates the news to create sensations and attract readers.

The news media are, above all else, in business to make money, but this is far from being a universally accepted reality. Many people cling to the notion that the members of the media are somehow the protectors of truth and justice. Others, including professional con artists, are aware that the media are neither objective nor consistently accurate. To a con artist this fact is neither good nor bad, it's just business.

What does concern con artists is the media's ability to influence or otherwise manipulate great numbers of people. If, for example, the media suddenly decided to place fraud into the category of *real crime*, then con artists, embezzlers, dishonest politicians, and a host of others would be forced to face the wrath of an informed public.

The absolute best you can ever hope to obtain from the media already exists. Their inconsistent coverage of your activities sends an unspoken message to all that fall prey to con games. The message says we don't have time or space to waste reporting on something so trivial as fraud when there's real crime to be exploited. Real crime is rape, murder, and mayhem. Real crime shocks the conscience. It's appalling, it's gruesome, and most of all—it sells.

The problem with the media concept of real crime is that it does not occur as often as they would have their customers believe. A more common occurrence is something the media call slow news days. In other words, those days when the likes of Jeffrey Dahmer and Theodore Bundy take the day off. Also excluded from the real-crime category are armed robberies in which no one is killed or any other crime that lacks the potential for shocking their readers or viewers into buying their product. What's new is not the media's main concern. Rather, it has become what's new and bad—really bad.

A word of caution: When peace and tranquility reach epidemic proportions the media will offer their customers a sacrificial substitute. Ply your trade on one of those days and you will pay dearly for your poor judgment.

Avoiding such foolish mistakes only requires a minor investment of your time. On arriving in a city, town, or village where you plan to operate, review the local news. If there are lots of stories about catastrophic or otherwise attention-getting events—such as floods, earthquakes, fires, political corruption, gang wars, and so on—then there exist plenty of diversions to cover your seemingly non-newsworthy activities. After you begin plying your trade and the news media makes it clear that they have discovered your scam, take this as a signal to move on to safer territory. Ignore this advice and you greatly increase your chances of being caught.

Book Buddies

Have you ever read a fraud prevention book? Do you know of anyone who has? You would be astounded to discover just how many fraud-related books and articles there are in existence. You would be equally impressed to learn just how many people don't read them.

Even avid readers seldom, if ever, think about doling out hard-earned cash for a book about fraud. Believing that such events are about as likely as being caught in a meteor shower, they simply cannot justify such an irresponsible investment of their time or money.

Occasionally, however, a book about fraud finds its way to Hollywood and is transformed into a movie. Although entertaining, these stories are usually fictional and grossly inaccurate. Confidence crimes are reduced to adventures, victims are cast as idiots, and by movie's end the con man gets the money, a beautiful woman, and a great vacation somewhere in southern France.

Before you think that it cannot get any better than this, here's one for the road. According to Charles E. O'Hara, the author of the widely distributed law enforcement training book, *Fundamentals of Criminal Investigation*, "The disturbing characteristic of most confidence games is the fact that the victim is knowingly engaging in an illegal act."

To further reduce confidence crimes to a category outside the realm of real crime, O'Hara added the following, "It is difficult to touch even lightly on this topic (confidence crime) without allotting to it a space in the crime world far out of proportion to the small number of persons who practice professionally the art of swindling." Although O'Hara probably never intended to include every act of fraud in the category of confidence crime, it would take a well-informed reader to assume otherwise. Then, too, if the readers were well informed they probably wouldn't be reading the book.

When viewing the assistance you shall receive during your career as a professional con artist, being arrested, convicted, and sentenced is an unlikely combination. Victims who refuse to report, media ignorance and outright manipulation of crime statistics, cops who don't know how or why any particular con game works, prosecutors who refuse to issue formal complaints, judges who dole out lenient sentences, and parole boards who are quick to release nonviolent criminals all help to make a con artist's career one of the most profitable, low-risk criminal ventures ever devised.

The Enemy

While the media are busy inventing reality for their customers there are other organizations that know exactly what con artists do for a living and how extensive their crimes are, and are busy doing everything in their power to stop them. The largest of these organizations are police fraud investigation teams, insurance companies, and financial institutions. Whenever you meet any serious resistance you can bet that it will come from one of these three sources.

Whatever the source, each possesses the ability to identify you, locate you, and hold you accountable for your misdeeds. Depressing as this might be, it is nevertheless a reality you must consider before entering the world of a professional con artist.

Criminal's Justice System

To end this chapter on a positive note, let's talk about prison. Having alluded to the possibility of being caught, now is a good time to put the matter in easy-to-digest terms.

Every con artist quoted or mentioned in the preceding chapters shares a common bond. Each of them possesses a lengthy criminal arrest record. These arrests, however, are nothing more than temporary inconveniences and should not be taken too seriously.

A good example of our justice system's infinite tolerance comes in the form of a well-known transient con artist who has been arrested on more than 127 occasions. In all she has spent no more than 30 days in jail and to this day continues to net a sizable tax-free criminal income. She long ago discovered that all the tough talk about "an all-out war on crime," or those politically motivated "get tough on crime" campaigns are not meant to include con games or other such nonviolent criminal activities.

Although at some point during your career as a con artist you will be arrested, the frequency of those arrests depends on how often you work, the number of mistakes you make, when and where you make those mistakes, and on the length of your career. Now for the sensitive topic—prison.

Although the words *arrest* and *prison* appear to be associated they are, at best, only distant cousins. More to the point, the odds are that being arrested, convicted, and sent to prison is an unlikely conclusion.

In all fairness I must note that *unlikely* is not synonymous with *never*. Even though the overall odds are in your favor, setting odds is hardly an exacting science and is dependent on a mixture of fact, chance, and pure speculation. In other words, serving time in prison is a possibility that will exist throughout your career. The good news is that you have many friends within the criminal justice system working hard to maintain your freedom.

To obtain a sample of the types of support you shall receive only requires that you visit any criminal court of your choosing. Without fail you will notice an addictive reliance on two concepts called plea bargaining and restitution.

Minus the glitter, plea bargaining is merely a polite euphemism for cutting a deal. It provides an escape route for anyone arrested and charged with a crime. This is how it works:

You are caught committing a serious crime. The police present their case to the district attorney who then decides if formal charges will be issued against you. If the case against you is solid, a case where there is more than sufficient evidence to prove your guilt, your attorney enters and negotiates a deal with the district attorney. The deal of choice often involves having you admit your guilt to a lesser offense. For example, if arrested for felony burglary your attorney will have the charge reduced to a misdemeanor theft. This greatly reduces the likelihood of your going to prison.

If you are guilty but the case against you is weak, your attorney will demand a jury trial. This tactic has several advantages.

For one, if every arrested suspect demanded a jury trial our courts would soon be overwhelmed and come to an immediate and complete halt. For another, setting up a jury trial takes time, and the more time the better. As every defense attorney knows well, stall the trial date and witnesses will forget details, lose interest, move away, and even die. Last, but not least, if your case does go to trial you still have a good chance of beating the system.

In the aftermath of the O. J. Simpson trial it should be very clear that confusing a jury is a fine art. Take 12 average citizens, expect them to understand legal principles that the attorneys themselves are not sure of, throw highly technical and scientific evidence at them, bore them senseless, and in the end they will have nothing to work from but pure emotion. This is why the closing arguments are so important. Without a clue about what they are doing the last thing a juror hears are the lawyer's interpretations of the evidence. The attorney who puts on the best performance wins.

Another path to freedom is called restitution. Restitution was originally intended to serve as a means of giving back what was taken from the victim, and was to be used along with other punishment. This companion process has since evolved into a form of legalized extortion wherein victims are presented with an ultimatum: Either they drop their complaint against the arrested criminal and accept the guaranteed return of their stolen property, or take their chances with a protracted court battle that will require a lot of their time and little chance of getting back what was stolen from them.

Now let's look at a worst-case scenario. You have just been arrested and stand a good chance of being tried, convicted, and sent to prison. What are your options?

- Hire an expensive lawyer (assuming that there is such a thing as an inexpensive one) and hope that he or she can convince a jury that you are not what you are.
- Post a percentage bond or bail. Add to it your promise to return for trial, and then flee the area posthaste.

That the courts would accept the promise of an accused con artist defies understanding, but they do it anyway. Incidentally, if you failed to choose option two, please do yourself a favor and stay honest.

As you can see, the criminal justice system is stacked in your favor. Unless you happen to err at a time when the courts must appease an angry mob of citizens, or you resort to using violence, being sent to prison is just not as easy as it once was. So relax!

CHAPTER NINE

FOR COPS ONLY

*"The only thing necessary for the triumph of evil
is for good men to do nothing."*
—Edmund Burke (1729-1797)

As an apprentice con artist you should now know how to get others to do your bidding. For example, if you wanted people to read a particular chapter of a book you were writing you might consider using a title that pretends to exclude them from its reading. Something like, "For Cops Only" might do the trick because it plays into their natural curiosity.

Having captured their attention you must then let it be known why they should continue to read. In the present case, I thought you should know what your potential enemies—the police—are up against whenever they entertain any thought of interfering with your career as a professional con artist.

For those readers who are law enforcement officers, I will waste no words on the difficulties involved with police work. As the citizens who pay our salaries see it—so what? If the job is too difficult, there is no law preventing us from seeking another profession. Having accepted the job, we agreed to keep our employers—the public—out of harm's way. For them, there is no middle ground. We either do what they hired us to do or we don't.

A DISPARAGING JOURNEY

It is not surprising that police officers throughout the country are discovering the depth of our nation's fraud and confidence-crime problems. Given the frequency at which these crimes are being committed, such a discovery is about as startling as finding out that not everyone plays by the rules.

Soon after recovering from a feeling of inadequacy for not having noticed the problem sooner, many of the officers embark on a mission to ferret out and destroy the con artists in their midst. What they will encounter during their journey is well documented by those who have gone before them. Let us look at some of the information they will likely find.

Discovery 1: Statistically speaking, fraud and confidence crimes do not exist. The U.S. Department of Justice, which gathers crime statistics from law enforcement agencies throughout the United States, publishes an annual Uniform Crime Report (UCR). Besides the many detailed statistics contained in this report there is also an illustration known as the "Crime Clock." The clock is not intended to imply a regularity in the commission of specific crimes; rather, it represents the annual ratio of crime to fixed time intervals. Included in the illustration are the following categories: Murder, forcible rape, robbery, aggravated assault, burglary, larceny-theft, (which includes shoplifting, pocket-picking, purse-snatching, thefts from motor vehicles, thefts of motor vehicle parts and accessories, bicycle thefts, etc.) and motor vehicle theft. Incidentally, the crimes listed appear in reverse order. The most serious offense, murder, occurs the least while the least serious, motor vehicle theft, occurs the most. Although the UCR notes the absence of any category for embezzlement, forgery, and con games, it lacks any explanation for the exclusion.

Interested in solving this mystery, in 1985 I conducted a national law enforcement survey. In all, 130 police departments from 29 states participated. What I discovered can be summed up in one sentence: The statistics on fraud and confidence crime exist, but are hopelessly buried under the generic category of theft.

All the survey participants were aware that fraud and confidence crimes were occurring within their jurisdiction. However, none of them could provide anything other than an educated guess as to their actual numbers. Even though bank-examiner frauds, pigeon drops, block hustles, and other confidence crimes were being reported, each report was listed under the heading of "theft from person." These reports were then batch-entered into the computer under the category of "larceny-theft." Extracting the data related to fraud and confidence crime would require countless hours of sifting through many thousands of reports. As you might have guessed, none of the survey participants expressed a desire to engage in such an arduous and boring task.

Discovery 2: Let there be no mistake, when an officer discovers just how prevalent confidence crimes really are he will naturally want to share his newfound knowledge with other officers.

What he is likely to be greeted with are blank stares and a lot of clichés. He will talk about multibillion dollar crimes; the other officers will answer with inconsistencies about statistics disproving their findings. He will point out the reality of fraud; the other officers will shake their heads patronizingly and mumble something about serious crime taking precedent over the trivial. After a while his excitement will fade and he will return to the reality of everyday life within a bureaucracy.

Discovery 3: Administrative response will be lukewarm. Misleading statistics coupled with limited police resources, public confusion, and competing pressure to address visible crime places fraud investigations solidly into the category of unnecessary and cost-prohibitive luxuries. And the con artists rejoice!

Discovery 4: Because fraud is so unstoppable, officers will eventually be asked to bring such investigative activities to an immediate and permanent halt. Although action is taken, it is—at best—only an exercise in how not to solve a problem.

With no sense of how the many different scams work, and no clue as to who is committing them, the chances of solving such offenses are nearly nonexistent. The only notable action resulting from the attempt is that it might force a few con artists to take a temporary vacation.

The usual pattern for this type of reactive enforcement works like this. Absent any consistent fraud prevention programs the con artists soon overwhelm the local populace. As more people become victims, demands are placed on the police to bring an end to the problem—or else!

The police respond by investing obscene amounts of money (yours) and other resources into the establishment of a special task force. Soon afterward the fraud problem - subsides and tranquility is restored. Insanity then prevails and the entire task force is disbanded, criminal intelligence records are destroyed, and officers are assigned to other duties. The con artists, of course, return with a vengeance soon after the task force is eliminated and the entire process is repeated—always at great expense to the community.

The Truth Be Told

Because I am about to instruct police officers on how to beat con artists at their own game, some explanation is in order. That I promised you information on how to become a professional con artist did not exclude anyone—including cops or your potential victims. But, you insist, this is an unfair double-cross. Is it?

Did I not, at the outset, say that I would deceive you whenever possible? Have I not repeatedly told you that there would be some risk involved? Then, too, let us not forget the constant mention of not trusting other con artists. If anything, you should consider this chapter as yet another learning tool intended to sharpen your deceptive skills. Furthermore, use it as a reminder that deception is not a one-way process reserved exclusively for those we so affectionately call con artists.

Honorable Deceptions

That you, as a police officer, should have to occasionally use a few of the con artist's tricks to control their activities is unfortunate, but necessary. When faced with a situation where fraud operates right under your nose, yet you are powerless to do anything about it, here's a proven method that is guaranteed to protect your community's citizens from harm.

If your department lacks a fraud investigation unit, create one. For a modest price you can easily purchase a self-adhesive placard that reads "Fraud Investigation Unit." Place the placard on your desk, the office door, or wherever you hang your hat. Set aside a filing cabinet and stencil on it the words "criminal intelligence records." At this point begin gathering as much information as you can about your local con artists. Join a fraud investigator's network, such as Professionals Against Confidence Crime, and place their criminal intelligence bulletins in a file marked "interstate con artists."

Outrageous, you say? Of course it's outrageous, if it were not then it couldn't possibly work. Because administrators are, believe it or not, only human, they dislike having to admit they do not know something. As such, they will observe your newly created fraud investigation unit and immediately assume that someone with higher authority approved the unit's creation. If you happen to work for a very small department and your only supervisor does ask what the signs are all about, don't panic. Just tell him or her that some prankster must be playing games. If successful, proceed to stage two.

Use the arrest of a con artist to your advantage. When informing your local news media about the arrest, casually but frequently interject the phrase, "our department's fraud investigation unit." Do this often enough and you can be certain that your department's unit will gain community-wide recognition. Also be sure to give your supervisors full credit. Whether they actually helped with the investigation and subsequent arrest makes little difference—give them credit anyway.

Think about it: What boss would chastise you for making him or her look good? In return you will obtain public recognition for your department's new unit and acceptance from your top administrator. From here on the unit will become as effective as you care to make it.

Making Life Miserable

Ensuring the survival of your newly established fraud investigation unit requires that you actually do damage to the con artists. Here's how it can be accomplished without any cost to your department.

Although no two fraud victims are alike, they nevertheless share in some common activities. For one, each must at some point during the scam—any scam—hand over their hard-earned cash. For another, and this is the most important part, the majority of them must obtain this cash from their financial institution. And herein lies the Achilles' heel to every scam ever devised.

Because almost every fraud victim, if given time to think, is smart enough to spot a scam, then it seems the solution to the fraud problem involves nothing more than finding a way to make them think. Believe it or not, this is not nearly as difficult as it seems. In fact, all that is required is a single sheet of paper containing some timely advice.

On the following page is a sample of a document now being used by financial institutions both in the United States and abroad. It is given to anyone who enters his or her financial institution with a demand for sizable amounts of cash, or whose transaction departs from usual banking patterns:

Since 1985 when my partner, Detective Neil Zuehlke, and I created this document, it has proven to be more than 85 percent effective. Although the communities that use this program still experience attempts by con artists who have yet to learn of this document's existence, there is a world of difference between almost losing one's life savings and an actual loss.

Conning the Cons

Ask any defense attorney what he hates most about his profession, and after listing clients who don't pay their bills he'll probably list clients who confess first and hire an attorney later. Why people confess to their crimes is a mystery to most, but for cops it's an everyday occurrence. Contrary to popular belief, cleansing one's soul is not the exclusive practice of first-time offenders. Hardened criminals and con artists alike readily confess to everything from thefts to murders.

An example of using trickery to encourage this soul-cleansing process occurred some years ago in a Midwestern

---

CASH WITHDRAWAL ALERT!

FOR YOUR OWN PROTECTION: BEFORE YOU WITHDRAW $_____IN CASH FROM YOUR ACCOUNT, PLEASE READ AND SIGN THIS FORM.

Consumers lose millions of dollars each year to con artists. Many scams involve the withdrawal of large amounts of cash from the customer's account. Before you withdraw money, consider the following:

- Have you received a call or met with someone claiming to be an FBI agent, bank examiner, police officer, detective or financial institution official? Do they want you to withdraw money to help in an investigation? Have they promised to return or deposit the money for you?

- Has anyone befriended you, then asked you to put up "good faith" money in order for you to share unexpectedly found money or valuables?

If the answer to any of these questions is yes, you may soon be the victim of a swindle. You may never see your money again. No financial institution conducts investigations by asking customers for help. No one will share money with you after getting your "good faith" dollars. However, these are common stories given by swindlers who mainly target older customers as victims.

REMEMBER, swindlers are nearly always friendly and have honest faces or pleasant, authoritative voices. This is how they gain your trust.

I have read and understand the above statement. By signing this form, I direct this financial institution to complete my request for cash withdrawal.

Teller _____   Customer _____

Financial Officer _____   Date _____

---

city after a team of con artists launched an all-out attack on the community's senior citizen population. Using the standard pigeon-drop scheme the duo managed to avoid capture while steadily adding thousands of dollars to their ill-gotten income. Through a fluke, the wife of one elderly victim happened to be driving by a local shopping center when she observed her husband entering a car occupied by an unknown man and woman. By the time she managed to negotiate her way into the crowded parking lot both her husband and the strangers had disappeared. Certain that her husband had been abducted, she called the police.

Shortly after broadcasting a description of the suspect's car, an alert detective spotted them in the parking lot of a nearby bank and immediately called for assistance. Minutes later both suspects became the temporary guests of the police department. I say temporary because absent any law preventing strangers from riding with older adults the suspects would soon gain their release.

On interviewing the elderly man, it was discovered that the suspects had offered to share with him some money they had found. He could not say why, but they had also asked him to show something they called "good faith money" before he could claim his part of the newfound booty. At last, the officers thought, we have our pigeon-drop suspects right where we want them. They were wrong.

Although the officers had probable cause to believe that the suspects were the con artists responsible for dozens of recent scams, they lacked any direct evidence linking them to the crimes. The previous victims could not identify them, the present victim was not at all clear about what had actually taken place, and without some solid evidence the suspects would have to be released.

Although neither suspect asked to be represented by an attorney, they made it clear that they knew how to play games. In other words, they had a pat answer for every question the detectives asked. Despite the weakness of those answers they were nevertheless sufficient to dampen the detectives' hopes of bringing this case to a successful close.

Unwilling to let these con artists off the hook without a fight, one of the detectives decided that a bit of strategic trickery was in order. While providing the suspects with the time to sit and think, the detective began assembling the props needed for his upcoming performance. The props consisted of a manila folder with the words "CONFIDEN-TIAL: CASE FILE" written across the top along with the name of the female suspect, Jane Smith. Inside this folder the detective placed several official-looking police reports that were topped off by a single sheet of paper marked "CONFESSION OF JANE SMITH."

The "confession form" briefly suggested that on questioning Jane Smith, she readily admitted to her part in each of the many schemes that had occurred during the past several months. Furthermore, it stated that her companion, John Doe, had forced her into committing the scams for repayment on money owed him, and that he had threatened to harm her children unless she agreed to help him.

The bottom of the form contained a summary written by the detective who conducted the questioning. The summary, in part read, "Subject appears to be truthful and is obviously concerned about the safety of her children. I recommend that John Doe be charged for all of the recent offenses and that the district attorney seek the maximum penalty allowed by law. Furthermore, that Jane Smith not be charged for these offenses unless she fails to provide testimony against John Doe."

Having prepared the folder, the detective instructed his partner to give him about 10 minutes alone with John Doe and then place a call into the interrogation room. On entering the interrogation room the detective placed his prop on a chair, making certain it was observable and within the suspect's reach. While attempting to convince the suspect about the importance of being honest, he was interrupted by what he treated as an irritating telephone call. "For Christ's sake, I'm busy," he yelled into the phone. "Can't anyone else take care of the problem?" He paused and then said, "OK, give me a minute." On hanging up the phone he apologized to John Doe, saying that he would have to leave the room for a few minutes to take care of some important business. Appearing distraught over the interruption, the detective "forgot" to take with him the folder marked CONFIDENTIAL: CASE FILE.

On his return to the interrogation room the detective again apologized for the interruption. He also noticed that the small wad of paper he had placed on top of the folder was now lying on the floor. Soon into the interview the suspect confessed, being careful not to say anything that would suggest he had pried into the detective's folder. His confession contained enough details to connect him and his partner to 17 offenses. Likewise, his partner confessed when discovering that the police suddenly knew every detail about her criminal escapades.

When the detective was asked by John Doe's attorney if he had shown his client any documents pertaining to the cases now before the court, the detective provided an honest answer and said no, he had not shown Mr. Doe any type of documents. The attorney, of course, knew what had happened, but was at an apparent loss on how to bring the information out in court without admitting that his client was not only a thief but was also guilty of prying into confidential documents. Even if the detective's resourcefulness had been exposed, it is unlikely that it would have been treated as anything other than a con artist being beaten at his own game.

A word of caution: Although the use of trickery has its benefits it can, at times, get you into trouble. This is especially true if such tactics are used to trick a suspect into waiving Miranda rights. Although the courts have ruled it legal to falsely tell a suspect that a victim identified him or that his fingerprints were found at the scene of a crime, such rulings are not cast in stone and are subject to change.

As a rule, spend some time with your local prosecutor and discuss, in detail, the fine art of legal trickery. When in doubt it is always best to err in favor of the suspect.

CHAPTER TEN

FINAL TRUTHS

"We must make the world honest before we can honestly say to our children that honesty is the best policy."
—George Bernard Shaw

The game ends here. Having seen life through the perspective of real-life con artists, we will now leave their world and examine what they have taught us—and what they failed to mention.

As you might already suspect, learning to lie professionally is not enough; with that you may only remain an ordinary liar all your days. You must also find pleasure in destroying everyone who crosses your path and acquire a genuine hatred for society's rules and everything else not of your own design. Without these desires, you will never possess the antisocial behavior of a predator. And let there be no doubt, con artists are among the most rapacious creatures in our society.

Remove the disguises used by, and created for, these purveyors of misery and you shall come face-to-face with a psychopath. Also called the antisocial personality by the

American Psychiatric Association, psychopaths are incapable of significant loyalty to individuals, groups, or social values. They are grossly selfish, callous, irresponsible, impulsive, and unable to feel guilt or learn from experience or punishment. Besides con artists, others included in this category are unprincipled business people, shyster lawyers, quack doctors, high-pressure evangelists, crooked politicians, impostors, drug pushers, mass murderers, and other assorted criminals.

Dr. Robert Hare, considered one of the world's foremost experts in psychopathy, provided a vivid description of this disorder in his book, *Without Conscience*:

> Psychopaths are social predators who charm, manipulate, and ruthlessly plow their way through life, leaving a broad trail of broken hearts, shattered expectations, and empty wallets. Lacking in conscience and in feelings for others, they selfishly take what they want and do as they please, violating social norms and expectations without the slightest sense of guilt or regret. Their bewildered victims desperately ask, "Who are these people?" [1]

Assigning such traits to con artists, Hare documented the most accurate description I have ever encountered. In fact, I have never met a con artist that did not possess the character deficiencies he describes:

> Given the glibness and facility with which they lie, it is not surprising that psychopaths successfully cheat, bilk, defraud, con, and manipulate people and have not the slightest compunction about doing so. They are often forthright in describing themselves as con men, hustlers, or fraud artists. Their statements reveal their belief that the world con-

sists of givers and takers, predators and prey, and that it would be foolish not to exploit the weaknesses of others.[2]

Viewing this emotional poverty helps to explain why con artists are not driven only by a desire to amass material wealth. Control over others and the opportunity to demolish someone's life provides a thrill that money just can't buy. Any admiration we hold for such creatures can, I hope, only be founded upon a misconception about their true character and a lack of understanding about the damage they leave in their wake.

If you believe this is an unfair characterization of really clever people who only engage in harmless acts of deception, then please return to the previous chapters. This time, compare how the con artists think, act, and speak, with the characteristics of a psychopath. If you discover anything resembling normalcy, then please consider such instances as either misprints or an unintentional oversight on my part.

WHY WE TOLERATE THE INTOLERABLE

We enter this world with about as much social charm as an ax murderer. We are complete egotists; selfish, greedy, and at the mercy of our emotions and wants. Without guidance from those who love and care for us, we would lack the social feeling that is intended to transform us into hard-working, unselfish, public-minded individuals who are willing to sacrifice our own interests for those of others.

There is little doubt that we all know altruistic individuals who are always available when we most need them. The examples of such unselfish devotion are in abundance and range from the ultimate sacrifice of one's life to save another to uncomplicated acts of kindness. Whatever the example, all of them serve to remind us of what it really means to be human.

Con artists, of course, see no sense in pleasing others and are content with living a hedonistic lifestyle. Realizing that we share with them this natural impulse to satisfy our wants and needs, and knowing that we, too, tell lies to get what we want, seldom are we willing to condemn them. Instead, we interpret their activities as a magnification of what everyone else is doing on an amateur level. While we openly denounce their behavior, there resides in us a little demon that causes us to silently envy their ability and willingness to break the rules.

We would cross the proverbial line into the realm of the professional liars, but those childhood no-nos that grew into thou shall nots somehow created in us a conscience. Were it not for the internal conflict between what we desire and what we must do, a conscience would be an unneeded thing. Regrettably, these opposing feelings coexist and force us to seek out ways to satisfy our wicked cravings while maintaining our morality.

The most convenient release comes in the form of books and movies depicting con artists as the aristocrats of the criminal world. Through these fictitious characters we safely wreak havoc on society before returning safely to our morally acceptable roles as honest, law-abiding citizens.

The only apparent harm in all this appears to occur on a subconscious level. We realize that fraud is a crime, but after being entertained by the likes of Robert Redford and Paul Newman (who in 1973 portrayed a pair of con men in the classic film, *The Sting*), we no longer view real thieves with as much disdain as they are due.

In 1976 the Ideal Toy Company even produced a board game based on *The Sting* for ages 10 to adult. The object of the game was to amass great wealth by conning (lying to) your opponents. The best liar reigned victorious after successfully dumping worthless property onto the laps of their now bankrupt opponents. Perhaps we are now ready for a game sequel called the Sesame Street Auto Theft game, or Barney The Burglar.

Comprehension Gone Astray

Throughout my entire law enforcement career I have heard well-intentioned individuals tell me that fraud pales in comparison to real crimes like robbery, murder, and rape. For them, fraud has no real victims, no serious consequences, and no impact on societal progress. Although this belief continues to gain support, we are now paying the price for such obstinately perverse thinking. The cost of this public opinion is erosion of the trust that is so crucial to the survival of a civilized society.

In a national survey conducted in 1996 by the Washington Post in conjunction with Harvard University and the Kaiser Family Foundation, it was disclosed that the majority of Americans no longer trust one another and have lost the once-accepted notion that most evildoers are safely behind prison walls. For reasons to be explained later in this chapter, this survey proves that our reasons to distrust others have increased, while the amount of trust we invest remains constant. If this were not true, fraud would become the first crime in the annals of criminal science to become extinct.

In Those We Trust

Con artists would like us to believe that trust is something best left to foolish and otherwise gullible dupes. Once again, they are not being entirely honest with us. This particular policy might fare well in the movies or other works of fiction, but it has no chance in the real world. All of us, including the most proficient con artists on Earth, are far more trusting than we realize.

But, as noted earlier, although we are no longer comfortable with placing *complete* trust in others, we have yet to devise a sensible way to avoid such an investment. We have neither the time nor the inclination to verify everything we hear and see. When we purchase groceries from the local market, we trust that they are safe to eat. If not, we would have to conduct chemical tests or return to the ancient practice of using human food tasters. When driving the family car over a bridge, we trust it was properly constructed and that we won't suddenly become proof of Newton's Law of gravity.

You can, I'm sure, add many hundreds of other instances that occur in the course of a normal day in which you must place your life in the hands of people you have never met. But this necessity to trust in others is not without controls.

In setting acceptable standards of conduct we have created laws, ordinances, and other regulations to protect us from harm. In theory, such controls provide a blueprint of our shared morals, values, and ethics. As of the writing of this book, those shared values have given way to radical individualism, confusion, and widespread public apathy. We have become increasingly tolerant and now accept the most outrageous conduct as little more than self-expression.

As former secretary of education (1985-1988) and President George Bush's "drug czar," William Bennet said in an article published in 1998 in *Imprimus* magazine, "Despite our wonders and greatness, we are a nation that has experienced so much social regression, so much decadence, in so short a period of time, that we have become the kind of place to which civilized countries used to send missionaries."

In demonstrating how far we have digressed, Bennett used the following example: "Social regression and decadence are glaringly obvious in the current presidential administration. Now, whenever I make a comment these days criticizing Bill Clinton, someone inevitably asks, 'Aren't you casting stones?' It shows how far we have fallen that calling upon the President of the United States to account for charges of adultery, lying to the public, perjury, and obstruction of justice is regarded as akin to stoning." The point here is that if we can't find it in ourselves to pass moral judgment on the leader of this nation, then our refusal to hold con artists accountable is understandable.

Former United States Court of Appeals judge Robert H. Bork attributes part of our moral decline to "fragmentation." In his book, *Slouching Towards Gomorrah*, he said, "A fragmented society, one in which a sense of community has disappeared, is necessarily a society of low morale. It displays a loss of nerve, which means that it cannot summon the will to suppress public obscenity, punish crime, resist the demands of self-proclaimed victim groups for preferential treatment, or maintain standards of reason and scholarship."

This rather bleak view of our situation is constructed on a solid foundation of easy-to-verify fact. You need only look at the insanity that occupies most of our daily news to get a sense of how far we have digressed. William Bennett added to this view when he said, "America is a place of heroes, honor, achievement, and respect. But is it also a place where heroism is often confused with celebrity, honor with fame, true achievement with popularity, individual respect with political correctness. Our culture celebrates self-gratification, the crossing of all moral boundaries, and now even the breaking of all social taboos."

It would seem that during all this confusion and moral decline we have developed a bad habit of investing our trust in all the wrong people. How this occurred is a topic for another day, but how we can protect against a continuance of this misplaced trust is not difficult and only requires the asking of two questions.

- Does the person giving me this information have anything to gain by lying to me?
- If this person is lying to me, how much will it affect my life?

Should the answer to either of these questions include the words *a lot*, then let this serve as your credibility guide. This might appear overly simplistic, but it does work. Any difficulty in using these questions will most likely occur when the person providing the information happens to be saying what you want to hear. And as you have observed in all of the con games presented in this book, telling suckers what they want to hear is paramount to the success or failure of the game.

To test this easy-to-use safeguard, you could apply it to me. What do I have to gain by lying to you, and if I am lying, what do you have to lose? I, of course, expect to become instantly wealthy from the sale of this book. If forced to be a bit more realistic, I will be sufficiently pleased to know that you and a handful of your family and friends read what I have written. And what do you stand to lose? Absolutely nothing. Your knowledge of fraud now surpasses most everyone else's in America, including cops.

The End Product

You will by now realize that even though I delivered on my promise to tell you how the various con games are played, it was never my intention to transform you into a psychopathic thief. I simply chose to put to good use what our nation's con artists have shown me, and to make less bad that which I cannot hope to eliminate. Any desire on your part to become a professional liar will have nothing to do with this book and everything to do with a deep-seated personality disorder. I can only encourage anyone afflicted with this deficiency to seek immediate psychiatric assistance.

Now would be a good time to let you in on another of my honest deceptions. The mechanics that go into the making of the con games we've examined are also contained in nearly every fraud prevention book ever written. You know, the books we talked about earlier, the ones few people read. Other how-to-sources include movies, novels, the news media, and television programs. In telling you how to protect yourself, it is oftentimes necessary to explain how the crimes are committed. Because the con artists who commit the crimes appear far more exciting than do the authors who write about their escapades, I chose to allow the cons to provide the guided tour while offsetting their rationalizations and glaring falsehoods with an ample amount of truth.

The most ludicrous source of information on frauds comes from con artists who become authors and advisors. After destroying countless men and women with their lies, they suddenly appear claiming to have seen the error of their ways. In return, we hire them as fraud prevention consultants and think nothing of paying for the honor of reading about the trusting souls they devastated during their career. One can only imagine how utterly stupid we appear to these psychopaths when we insist on being fleeced by admitted con artists, and of our willingness to pay for the privilege.

Help Is Not On the Way

If spending some time in the gutter with these antisocial parasites sickened you, and there now exists an expectation that your local police will bring fraud to a sudden halt, then you will depart this world as a disappointed soul. And here's why.

In a 1995 survey, 72 Canadian police chiefs were asked to explain their noted inability to effectively investigate and prosecute fraud and other white-collar crime cases. The chiefs were allowed to list multiple reasons for their departments' problems, and cited the following:

Lack of trained resources:	47 percent
Lack of financial resources:	49 percent
Insufficient evidence:	29 percent
Other:	22 percent

Survey participants also concluded that in the near future, corporations would have to use private resources to investigate cases involving fraud. The reasons for this included the complexity of the crimes committed, insufficient investigative expertise within their departments, and a lack of priority being placed on the investigation of white-collar crimes. All of this despite the belief among 89 percent of the police chiefs that fraud would increase.

Although this survey was conducted in Canada, my law enforcement contacts in the United States assure me that the results would be identical here. Fraud is not a high priority with the police because it's not a high priority with the customers. And the customers are you and everyone else who relies on the police to keep them out of harm's way.

After three decades of life within a bureaucracy, I can say with the utmost confidence that nothing gets done until sufficient numbers of citizens like you get mad. When this occurs, the impossible suddenly becomes achievable, and the once-ignored problems mysteriously become non-problems. Whether or not such an uprising occurs depends on how much more tolerance the American public is willing to expend. Perhaps if we stop to consider the mess we are leaving our children, our tolerance will dissipate and we shall become less apathetic and more involved in dealing with those who insist on bringing out the worst in all of us.

If you need something to get mad about, consider this. Your local law-enforcement agency could easily prevent most of the frauds now occurring in your community. All that is needed is an understanding of how the various frauds work, a handful of trained officers, and very little money. As was noted in the Canadian survey, most administrators know that a problem exists, but wrongly assume that the cure requires resources they don't have. More important, they really believe no one cares about the problem, so why bother.

Although this book focused on con artists, the list of others who intentionally mislead and lie to us grows with each passing day. Even more upsetting than this is our willingness to accept, without a challenge, the most outrageous and often asinine views ever set forth. Minus the polite euphemisms, if we insist on playing the part of village idiots, then we have no right to complain when we are viewed and treated as such.

Yes, we all tell lies of one degree or another, and possess selfish desires. We also do stupid things from time to time, say things we don't mean, treat others unfairly, and become so full of ourselves that we begin to believe the world would end in our absence. Unless this foolhardy activity becomes a daily routine, or we are unable to recognize our shortcomings, there is no reason for us to compare our activities with that of a psychopath.

If, by chance, you possess the traits of a predator and believe it would be foolish not to exploit the weaknesses of others, then you have earned the right to consider yourself a unique, albeit useless, individual. And let there be no doubt in your mind, the only worthwhile contribution you shall ever make will consist of the only thing you cannot cheat—your death.

1. Hare, Robert D. *Without Conscience: The Disturbing World of the Psychopaths Among Us.* New York: Pocket Books, 1993.
2. Ibid.

BIBLIOGRAPHY

Abagnale, Frank W., with Stan Redding. *Catch Me If You Can.* New York: Grosset & Dunlap, 1980.

Berne, Eric, M.D. *What Do You Say After You Say Hello?* New York: Grove Press, Distributed by Random House.

Bork, Robert H. *Slouching Towards Gomorrah.* New York: Reagan Books, Harper Collins, 1996.

Brannon, W.T. *The Con Game and "Yellow Kid" Weil.* New York: Dover Publications, Inc., 1974.

Carson, Robert and James Butcher. *Abnormal Psychology and Modern Life.* New York: Harper Collins Publisher, 1992.

Erdnase, S.W., M.D. *The Expert at the Card Table: The Classic Treatise on Card Manipulation.* Dover Publications, 1995.

Hare, Robert D. Dr. *Without Conscience: The Disturbing World of the Psychopaths Among Us.* New York: Pocket Books, 1993.

KPMG Investigation and Security Inc. *1995 Police Chief's Survey Report.* Toronto, Canada pp. 2-16

Lewis, Steven. *Time Binding Ethics, 1996.* (lewis@kcmetro.cc.mo.us)

Lindberg, Gary. *The Confidence Man in America.* New York: Oxford University Press, 1982.

Marlock, Dennis and John Dowling. *License To Steal, Traveling Con Artists, Their Games, Their Rules—Your Money.* Boulder, Colorado: Paladin Press, 1994.

Maurer, David W. *The Big Con: The Story of the Confidence Man and the Confidence Game.* Indianapolis: Bobbs-Merrill, 1940.

O'Hara, Charles E. *Fundamentals Of Criminal Investigation.* Illinois: Charles C. Thomas Publisher, 1977.

Wharton, Don. "Five Frauds To Watch Out For." *Reader's Digest*, March 1955, pp. 101-104.

About the Author

Lieutenant Dennis Marlock recently retired from the Milwaukee Police Department, where he spent most of his 31-year career investigating frauds and confidence crimes. He cofounded and currently oversees the daily operation of Professionals Against Confidence Crime, an international law enforcement organization. He is known throughout the United States as an expert on fraud prevention, and he has written two books and numerous articles on fraud and transient con artists.

CONGRATULATONS! YOU HAVE JUST PURCHASED HOME AIR'S MOST FUEL EFFICIENT, EASY TO OPERATE, EASY TO ASSEMBLE AIRCRAFT.

XRT-Assembly Instructions

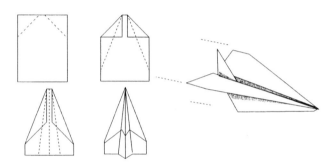

THE PLANE
- Flip the paper over so that the printed fold lines are facing down.
- Turn the corners back to the outside fold lines and crease. Repeat for the next set of folds.
- Fold up along the center line so text is inside and graphics are on the outside.
- Finally fold down each wing.

FLIGHT INSTRUCTIONS
(1) Hold lower half of the aircraft in your hand. (2) Using a brisk forward motion, throw the plane and release it into the air. (3) The XRT-7 is equipped with automatic pilot and requires no further piloting skills on your part.

MATERIALS LIST:
Additional material need to duplicate the assembly of the XRT-7 can be obtained from any paper supply store. Please do your part to protect our environment and use recycled paper. Thank You.